INTO *the* WILD

A Unique Devotional for the Outward-Thinking Teen

Charles Mills

Cover design: Brandon Reese
Cover design resources: Getty.com
Interior design: Aaron Troia

You can obtain additional copies of this book by calling toll-free 1-800-765-6955 or by visiting AdventistBookCenter.com.

ISBN 978-0-8163-6748-1

May 2022

Contents

Welcome!

This book is about you. Yes, *you*—as imperfect, mistake-ridden, hopelessly nerdy, or totally confused about life as you may be.

How do I know who you are? Because I was you once. I looked out at this world and said, "What an absolutely messed up place! How am I supposed to live in that?"

Thankfully, I had help. Parents, teachers, friends, and various church members taught me the basics for surviving in this dangerous world. I read inspiring books, watched faith-lifting television programs, and hung out with really smart people who eagerly offered advice on how to make it through each day. I recognize that you may not have these same opportunities.

Well, I'm not your dad or your teacher, and I don't attend the church where you worship each week. But I want to be your friend. And I'd be honored to spend a few moments with you during the coming weeks or months, offering ideas for how to make your life happier, healthier, and more digestible.

How do I plan to do that? By introducing you to Someone you may not fully know—yet. Someone who really does have all the answers, who actually can save you from the dangers ahead, and who's in a position to promise you a future beyond your imagination.

My goal throughout this book is to turn your thoughts outward, help you see the needs around you, and point out the incredibly powerful weapons available to you as you fight your personal battles with evil and evildoers.

This devotional is as unique as you are. It's not carved up into daily offerings. Instead, I invite you to find a few moments from time to time to check out one or two of the often bite-size, to-the-point pieces. I know you're busy. I just want to be there when you need a quick refresher on things like why you exist and what God has to offer. I think you'll be pleasantly surprised and, hopefully, encouraged as you do battle with the dark forces all around us.

Of course, some of you may read this book from cover to cover in just a couple of sittings. That's OK too. I'll do my best to keep up.

So, why did I write this book? The answer is simple. We're in the middle of an ongoing conflict for our very souls. We need all the help we can get!

Oh, and one more thing. You're almost an adult. Thus, I'm going to treat you like one and present my thoughts to you as if I'm sharing with someone who can think deeply and wants truth presented in a mature, practical way. No kids' stuff here. This is serious!

So, buckle up, my friend. We're taking this journey together. Turn the page, and let's head out . . . into the wild!

PART 1

PLAN B

*In the God-versus-Satan conflict,
the battle is all about you.*

Voices

"My sheep listen to my voice; I know them, and they follow me."
—John 10:27

I begin this devotional book much as I've begun most things in my life—not knowing exactly how it will end. Oh, I know how I *want* it to end. I've outlined the main subjects and what I want to accomplish for you. But the distance between desire and reality can sometimes be rather wide, as you've probably discovered for yourself during the past few years.

That's OK. I've lived long enough to know that such a distance isn't necessarily a bad thing. It's simply another challenge we all must overcome.

So, here you are, trying to get through your teen years in one piece thinking the same thing: *How will it end? How will I ever make it through the next week or month or even today?*

Well, I'd like to help. As I said earlier, I want you to become very familiar with Someone who can see the end from the beginning and help you connect those sometimes-confusing dots.

But don't think for one minute that God's going to do the hard work for you. Instead, picture Him as your Coach running along the sidelines, shouting instructions, trying to be heard over the roar of the crowd as you twist, turn, and weave your way through the obstacles coming at you from all sides. *You're* in the game. *You're* running the plays. Success is up to *you*, but you must pay attention to your Coach.

So, how do you separate His voice from the millions of other voices shouting in your ear from the grandstand of life? More to the point, how do you know when it's God speaking to you and not the devil? Good question! Sometimes the devil does a pretty good impersonation of God. Sometimes people around you insist that the devil's voice *is* the voice of God.

Well, let me ask you a question. How do you pick your friends' voices out of a crowd? "It's easy," you might say. "I know what they sound like. I've listened to them many times before. I love them."

Bingo.

* * * * *

What About Me?

"I will ascend above the tops of the clouds;
I will make myself like the Most High."

—Isaiah 14:14

You've heard the story: perfect heaven filled with perfect angels doing perfect things for the perfect beings scattered across the vast, perfect universe. Overseeing it all? A perfect God. Love ruled the day. All was peace and happiness. But that didn't end well. Why?

For love to exist, there has to be choice. You can't force love, demand it, or "arrange" for it to happen. You don't say to someone in whom you're interested, "Love me, or I'll beat you up." True love is the result of someone making a freewill choice. At that moment in history, everyone was choosing love—even Lucifer.

Then something happened. Over the course of time (we have no idea how long), this perfect heavenly being began to turn his thoughts inward. He watched as the other angels happily hurried about praising God, worshiping God, and singing songs about God.

Then one day a peculiar thought took root in his perfect angel brain. It was just a fleeting impulse, but it left a mark. In a moment of quiet introspection, Lucifer thought to himself, *What about me?*

He could ask himself that question because of the free will built directly into love. He was free to think anything he wanted to think, to do anything he wanted to do, to believe any way he wanted to believe. No one was forcing him to worship God.

In time, that peculiar thought grew into an obsession. "I will ascend to the heavens," he decided. "I will raise my throne above the stars of God; I will sit enthroned on the mount of assembly" (Isaiah 14:13).

Today, we live in a world built by the choices that angel made. Our sorrows and pains are a direct result of the freedom baked into true love. The good news is that there's an alternative way to live. We can break the cycle of sin and sorrow. We just have to be prepared to fight a few battles. To be brutally honest, we need to be prepared for all-out war!

* * * * *

It's a War out There!

Then war broke out in heaven. Michael and his angels fought against the dragon, and the dragon and his angels fought back.

—Revelation 12:7

Satan (the dragon), filled with thoughts of himself, convinced one-third of the angels (Revelation 12:4) that God (Michael) was a tyrant, a bully, someone not to be trusted. His smear campaign began with whispers softly spoken and ended in open rebellion.

Now, before you begin envisioning columns of holy angels amassing on some heavenly battlefield to face off against other columns of rebel angels bent on taking over the throne of God, keep in mind that this was a battle of *attitudes*. The weapons were minds and thoughts, not smart bombs and semiautomatic rifles.

This battle—this war—pitted one conception of the character of God against another. One side announced, "God is love!" The other insisted, "God is mean, vindictive, and selfish." This set the theme for a battle between good and evil that continues to this day. Even Christ asked His disciples, "Who do you say I am?" (Matthew 16:15). How they answered told Him whether His messages of love and forgiveness were getting through.

Make no mistake; there's a war going on, and you are on the front lines. Each day, God says to you, "Who do you say I am? Am I mean, vindictive, and selfish? Am I who so many say I am? Or am I love?" How you answer—how you represent Him to the world—indicates how successful He's been in getting through to you.

As you head out into the wild today, remember for whom you're fighting. Choose your attitude weapons wisely. Arm yourself from the arsenal of truth, forgiveness, and acceptance. Then stand your ground in love.

* * * * *

Consequences

The great dragon was hurled down—that ancient serpent called the devil, or Satan, who leads the whole world astray. He was hurled to the earth, and his angels with him.

—Revelation 12:9

God had an interesting way of dealing with Satan after he—along with his supporters—rose up in rebellion against Him. It runs contrary to the way God is portrayed in much of the Old Testament and from many church pulpits today. There was no flash of lightning, no laser beam disintegrating the armies of evil, no boiling cauldron into which the antagonist was tossed.

No. After repeated attempts to bring them back into the fold of love, God reacted in a very unhuman way. He *hurled* them out of heaven—which is a dramatic way of saying, "He told them to leave and provided the transportation." Unfortunately for us, they ended up here, on Earth.

When you rebel against God, He will honor your choice. But first, He will try to draw you back to Him. If you persist in your rebellion, there will be consequences. Here, many people think of fire and brimstone, eternal punishment, and endless suffering. They picture God's rage and wrath. However, God is thinking of *separation.*

That's the consequence of sin:

> But your iniquities have separated
> you from your God;
> your sins have hidden his face from you,
> so that he will not hear (Isaiah 59:2).

In your journey into the wild today, don't fear for one moment that God has left you. If He seems far away, you're the one who's moved. If that's the case, what are you waiting for? Hurry back to His arms! He loves you. He wants to help you. He's waiting to forgive you.

* * * * *

The Application of Sin

The LORD God took the man and put him in the Garden of Eden to work it and take care of it.

—Genesis 2:15

Imagine this world before humankind sinned. It must have been amazing. Don't forget; sin was already here in this perfect world. But human beings hadn't discovered it, welcomed it, and decided to live by its rules yet. The earth was still as God intended it to be.

There was no need for forgiveness because no one did anything wrong. Fear?

What was that? No police officers, medical practitioners, trauma surgeons, judges, lawyers, or undertakers. There was just the Creator God, a man named Adam, and a garden.

And Satan.

What I'm trying to say is, Satan's presence doesn't mean anyone has sinned, just as that container of rat poison under the kitchen sink doesn't mean anyone or anything is going to die of rat poisoning. Sin is the *application* of Satan's principles in someone's life.

Living in the wild doesn't mean we have to be active sinners. Like Adam—and later Eve—we can live our lives using a much higher standard. We can take care of this planet—and everything on it—by supporting and participating in environment-saving projects. We can use our talents to bless others, serve others, and introduce others to God. We can actively reflect God's true character of love in our relationships with those around us.

The Garden of Eden represented life without sin, even though sin existed. It's the kind of world God wishes for each of us today—a world where He still has a say in our lives. When we're kind and considerate—when we turn our attention from ourselves to others—we're re-creating Eden and the life we were designed to live. We're living proof that this is God's world, in spite of the presence of the enemy.

I challenge you, my friend. Even though you're standing right in the middle of the wild, look for opportunities to prove to your friends that this is God's world.

* * * * *

The Right to Be

Then the LORD God made a woman from the rib he had taken out of the man, and he brought her to the man.

—Genesis 2:22

The message of the Bible is crystal clear. Women and men are basically made of the same stuff. Besides, there's no way any male should ever feel superior to any female because, truth be told, before man had a rib, he was mud.

Let me ask you a silly question. How many of you would become so angry with your hand—because it stole a candy bar from a store shelf—that you'd beat it to a pulp with a hammer? You wouldn't because that hand is part of you. You don't damage yourself. You protect yourself. Well, guess what, men? Women are part of you. We're all one creation. We can't be separated. And guess what, women? You and men are more alike than you even realize.

Four thousand years after Eden, a Bible writer reminded us, "Nor is there male and female, for you are all one in Christ Jesus" (Galatians 3:28).

Out there in the wild, some people insist that females are not equal to males. This attitude creates inequality in workplaces, sports, government, churches, and many homes. But we know better. In Eden, God was making a point. We're all equal!

That's why, if you're a guy, you approach girls with respect and thoughtfulness, just as you're respectful and thoughtful of yourself. If you're a girl, you never think of yourself as inferior or destined to live under the control of anyone but you. You have the same right to be who you are as he has to be who he is. End of story!

This is an important point because everything God has ever done—or ever will do—is for both sexes. His salvation, His sacrifice, and His promises are meant for all.

* * * * *

Job 1

God blessed them [Adam and Eve] and said to them, "Be fruitful and increase in number; fill the earth and subdue it. Rule over the fish in the sea and the birds in the sky and over every living creature that moves on the ground."

—Genesis 1:28

Ever wonder why you're here on Earth? Ever wonder what God wants you to do? Keep in mind that when God told Adam and Eve to be fruitful, multiply, fill, subdue, and rule, sin had yet to infect their lives, so certain words didn't carry the meaning they do now.

"Be fruitful and increase in number" is easy. Make families who can enjoy this beautiful world with you. Use your creative powers to do what I just did—make human beings.

"Fill the earth and subdue it." Use this earth in ways that will benefit both you and nature. *Subdue* simply meant "nurture it for your joy as well as the happiness of generations to come."

"Rule over the fish . . . birds . . . and every living creature." God was inviting Adam and Eve to "rule" the way He rules—in love and kindness, acting as a provider and supporter of all things natural. His "rule" is love.

This world and everything in it was created for men and women to enjoy, to learn from, to support through their skills and talents. Sin hadn't yet gripped the hearts of God's creatures. There was no survival of the fittest, no selfishness, no death, pain, or suffering. There was only love and the incredible creative powers that a caring God had planted in *everything* that moves and grows. It was God's home, freely shared with those who inhabited it. Adam and Eve were assigned as governors to watch over God's creation.

But something happened—something horrible—and everything changed. That's why God quickly moved to plan B for humankind. Yes, God had a plan B, and today, you and I are part of it.

* * * * *

A Devil by Any Other Name

Now the serpent was more crafty than any of the wild animals the LORD God had made.

—Genesis 3:1

I have a question for you: Why would any animal need to be "crafty" in Eden? The King James Version of the Bible uses the word "subtil," and *The Message* paraphrase identifies him as "clever." These words hint that this creature was up to something it didn't want anyone else to know about.

Continuing, we read, "He said to the woman, 'Did God really say, "You must not eat from any tree in the garden"?' " (Genesis 3:1).

OK. Reality check. We've got ourselves a talking snake here! But Eve didn't miss a beat. "The woman said to the serpent, 'We may eat fruit from the trees in the garden, but God did say, "You must not eat fruit from the tree that is in the middle of the garden, and you must not touch it, or you will die" ' " (verses 2, 3). It seems Eve had listened in class. She'd heard and remembered God's words.

Keep three things in mind. First, Satan will come at you using special skills and talents. He's so good at surprising people and appearing amazing that you won't even flinch if he shows up in some out-of-the-ordinary, even unreal way—like a talking snake.

Second, Satan always, *always* wants you to question God. That's the main theme of his attack on humankind.

Third, he lowered the boom on Eve with his favorite mode of operation. " 'You will not certainly die,' the serpent said to the woman" (verse 4). In other words, Satan loves to call God a liar.

During your journey into the wild today, if someone or something insists that God is wrong, mistaken, or not being totally open and honest with you, flash back to this moment. And realize that you've got yourself a talking snake.

* * * * *

Eye-Opening

When the woman saw that the fruit of the tree was good for food and pleasing to the eye, and also desirable for gaining wisdom, she took some and ate it.
—Genesis 3:6

Gaining wisdom? Who said that? "For God knows that when you eat from it your eyes will be opened, and you will be like God, knowing good and evil" (Genesis 3:5). These words of Satan the serpent should speak volumes to us today. Who doesn't want to be smart, clever, and insightful? Apparently, if you're smart, clever, and insightful, you don't need God and all His silly, hard-to-understand, and even-harder-to-follow rules and regulations. All you need is *you*!

Sound familiar? Sin is a longtime advocate of self-rule. It teaches that you'll survive if you're the fittest in the group. And be sure to watch out for number one! This concept goes against what God had in mind for us and runs contrary to how nature works.

Life is all about give-*and*-take. Plants draw in carbon dioxide and give off oxygen, which animals then draw into their lungs and convert to carbon dioxide, which the plants need to make oxygen. If ponds or lakes don't allow some of their waters to flow away as they welcome new rains, they stagnate. Even love requires give-and-take, or it's not love. It quickly becomes selfishness and, eventually, hate.

Satan was right about one thing. Going against God's original plan for humankind does tend to open the eyes. Those who eat forbidden fruit certainly learn all about evil, even though they were created to enjoy good. Some things, my friend, are better left unlearned. But, sadly, Eve chose the fruit—and the consequences it brought.

Today in the wild, you might come across some "fruit" of your own. It will look so good and pleasing to your eye. It may promise you incredible things—fame, fortune, sex appeal, even endless romantic love. I invite you to take a lesson from Eve's big mistake and quickly and prayerfully move on.

* * * * *

"Where Are You?"

She [Eve] also gave some [fruit] to her husband,
who was with her, and he ate it.

—Genesis 3:6

Well, of course, Adam ate the fruit Eve offered him! He'd bought into the serpent's song and dance routine too. Besides, he didn't want Eve to have all of that wonderful knowing and gaining. He wanted his eyes to be opened as well! They were, and what they saw was shocking. "Then the eyes of both of them were opened, and they realized they were naked; so they sewed fig leaves together and made coverings for themselves" (Genesis 3:7).

Out there in the wild without God, we are truly vulnerable. We are totally at risk. Yes, we're *naked.* So, we quickly find ways to hide our shame, cover our mistakes, and conceal our transgressions. We cower behind lies and anger. We build barriers to protect our inner selves. We become someone we weren't created to be. And, as is often the case, the first person to fall victim to our newfound uncertainty is us.

Continuing on, we read, "Then the man and his wife heard the sound of the LORD God as he was walking in the garden in the cool of the day, and they hid from the LORD God among the trees of the garden. But the LORD God called to the man, 'Where are you?' " (Genesis 3:8, 9).

Interesting thing about the wild: not only is it the devil's playground but also it's where God spends a lot of His time looking for us. He's not afraid to mingle with sinners and fruit-eaters. He's not afraid of snakes—even talking ones. He loves us even when we're cowering in our hiding places. "He [Adam] answered, 'I heard you in the garden, and I was afraid because I was naked; so I hid' " (verse 10).

It seems we've just uncovered another attribute of sin. Fear.

* * * * *

The Blame Game

And he [God] said, "Who told you that you were naked?
Have you eaten from the tree that I commanded you not to eat from?"
—Genesis 3:11

Busted!

Adam and Eve responded to God's questions concerning their behavior just as human beings have been responding to God for millennia:

> The man said, "The woman you put here with me—she gave me some fruit from the tree, and I ate it."
> Then the LORD God said to the woman, "What is this you have done?"
> The woman said, "The serpent deceived me, and I ate" (Genesis 3:12, 13).

"The devil made me do it." "It's your fault." "This is on you, not me." "I'm the victim here!" Or perhaps, "It's [choose one: my upbringing, my genes, my personality, my home life]." "It's circumstances." "It's fate." "I've been framed!"

I have a suggestion. When you're out there in the wild, don't make excuses for your blunders and bad judgments. Simply say, "Oops. That was wrong. I shouldn't have done that! My bad. My fault. My mistake." Believe it or not, things will probably come out better for you in the long run if you do.

I've often wondered what would have happened if Adam and Eve had confessed instead of pointed fingers. Would we be where we are today? If we've learned anything from reading the Bible, it's that God is a very, very forgiving Being. He'll go to incredible lengths to help reconstruct lives after people have stumbled headfirst into sin.

I guess we'll never know. Adam and Eve made their decision. They'd pinned their allegiance on Satan. And the consequences would be far-reaching.

However, we know better. We know that when we fall, God is there to catch us if we'll just be open and honest with Him and admit our mistake. Talk to Him, even if your lips are still moist from the juice of the apple.

* * * * *

Enmity

"And I will put enmity
between you and the woman,
and between your offspring and hers;
he will crush your head,
and you will strike his heel."

—Genesis 3:15

When God spoke of the natural consequences of sin to the serpent, Adam, and Eve that day in Eden (you can read the whole list in Genesis 3), He addressed Satan first. God knew where sin came from. He knew the source of all things evil. Adam and Eve had chosen to eat the forbidden fruit and follow Satan's lead, and now they were learning where that action—and their failure to seek forgiveness—were taking them. It wasn't a pretty sight.

One of the curses that God lowered on Satan is significant in my mind. This "enmity" (verse 15) that God placed in the woman's and the man's hearts should provide a ray of hope to everyone living in the wild.

The word *enmity* means "the state or feeling of being actively opposed or hostile to someone or something."* That's right. God placed in Earth's first inhabitants—and in you and me via our genetics—a "state or feeling of being actively opposed . . . to someone or something" when we come up against evil.

That's why when we're tempted to do wrong—to follow Satan's lead, to live by his rules—something kicks in deep inside of us. Something creates a sense of friction, animosity, even hostility toward that action. We somehow know that what we're about to do—what we're thinking or planning—is outside of God's ideal for us. Some call it conscience. I call it enmity, and I'm glad it's there.

Oh, sure, some cover it up with addictive habits that alter their ability to think and reason clearly. Some overpower it with pleasure seeking and an endless stream of excuses. But that's not you. You and I depend on our individual internal enmity to help guide us to safer shores.

So, if you face a choice today and can't seem to shake an uneasiness about heading in a certain direction or doing a certain thing, stop and thank God for the enmity in you. And respond accordingly.

* * * * *

* *Oxford English Dictionary*, s.v. "enmity (n.)," Lexico, accessed February 16, 2022, https://www.lexico.com/en/definition/enmity.

"It's Time"

So the Lord God banished him [Adam] from the Garden of Eden to work the ground from which he had been taken.
—Genesis 3:23

B*anished.* What a sad word! It means you can no longer be where you want to be.

Can you imagine Adam and Eve standing at the Garden's guarded gate, peering past the flaming swords of the cherubim (Genesis 3:24) at the flowers and trees and animals they knew and loved? Can you imagine their sorrow over what they'd lost?

But there's another scene I want you to imagine. In your mind's eye, notice God the Creator in the Garden looking at the two beings He formed to be His forever friends. Sin had separated them. Sin had driven them apart. God's love had allowed Adam and Eve to follow their own path, to go their own way, to attach their allegiance to their champion. They had, of their own free will, passed the governorship of this world to Satan. I think it's safe to say that there was great sorrow on both sides of the Garden's gate that day.

Earth's first humans had now entered the wild. They'd chosen to follow the serpent into a world filled with anger, disease, and death. Imagine what it was like when the couple watched the first flower die or when a bird fluttered to the ground at their feet, never to rise again. Their garden home was gone, replaced by a world where everything took without giving, where only the strong survived, where selfishness and hatred found fertile soil.

I also want you to imagine the Creator, Jesus, looking toward the sky and whispering to the Father He knew was listening, "It's time."

That announcement set in motion a plan that would change everything. That statement began a series of events that would, eventually, end the separation forever.

* * * * *

Restoration

He has saved us and called us to a holy life—not because of anything we have done but because of his own purpose and grace. This grace was given us in Christ Jesus before the beginning of time.

—2 Timothy 1:9

That plan B was always there, waiting to be implemented, just in case.

You see, God understood the risks associated with love and the freedom it guarantees; the same freedom the angels enjoyed before a third of them—and their leader, Satan—got themselves hurled out of heaven. True, pure, unsoiled love can be vulnerable. But God the Creator and His Father knew that their brand of love could outlast, outshine, and outperform sin. They understood that the same love that lets go can also reclaim. That's exactly what They planned to do.

Adam and Eve's choice to live by Satan's rules had severed the bond between God and humankind. So, the Creator and His Father put in motion their plan to reconnect with their lost friends, to rejoin them in "the cool of the day" (Genesis 3:8), to restore what was lost. How would they do that? By proving, beyond a doubt, that Satan was dead wrong, that God's way is the best way to live. "For the wages of sin is death, but the gift of God is eternal life in Christ Jesus our Lord" (Romans 6:23).

Thus began a campaign of restoration. You know the stories: a worldwide flood with the opportunity for salvation (only eight people responded). There were promises to Abraham, Moses leading a nation through a desert, and the setting up of the kingdom of Israel. There were prophets, teachers, rulers, and men and women of great faith battling men and women of none.

There were times of victories and defeats, moments of plenty and famine, and years of peace and war, all tied directly to how closely God's people followed what they knew to be right.

And finally, we see a road-weary man and a very pregnant woman approaching a town called Bethlehem. Plan B was about to get very personal.

* * * * *

In a Land Called Holy

So Joseph also went up from the town of Nazareth in Galilee to Judea, to Bethlehem the town of David, because he belonged to the house and line of David. He went there to register with Mary, who was pledged to be married to him and was expecting a child.

—Luke 2:4, 5

There's something surreal about planning a vacation that sounds like the travel itinerary of a disciple. Imagine a tour guide checking his clipboard and saying, "On our way to Jerusalem, we'll stop by Jericho. Tomorrow, after spending the morning in Bethlehem, we'll head north to Nazareth and then check out the synagogue in Capernaum on the shores of the Sea of Galilee." See what I mean? I actually did that!

A three-year stretch of my life was spent in the land many call "holy." Our home in Beirut, Lebanon, overlooked that capital city and the Mediterranean Sea. Our stay proved peaceful and enjoyable, even though a few months were spent in exile as we tried to escape the infamous Six-Day War that erupted in 1967.

While living in that part of the world, I discovered something intriguing. Anyone searching for Jesus can find small glimpses of Him in the Holy Land.

My first encounter took place on a barren, rocky hillside outside of the ancient city of Bethlehem. It was there that I began to realize that Jesus wasn't simply a character in a book or motion picture but an actual flesh-and-blood Person. Two thousand years ago, in that rugged, windswept, unforgiving land, the Creator of the universe made His first appearance as a human being.

No, He didn't show up as a brilliant light or caped superhero. Instead, He waved tiny pink fingers from a rough-hewn, straw-packed manger as a helpless infant. The Son of God—the very One who had brought the universe, this world, and Adam and Eve into existence—had willingly stepped into the wild. Why?

* * * * *

Lost Truth

Be alert and of sober mind. Your enemy the devil prowls around like a roaring lion looking for someone to devour.

—1 Peter 5:8

A lot had happened during the four thousand years since the gates of the Garden of Eden clanked shut behind Earth's first wayward couple. Humankind, out on its own, hadn't fared so well. There'd been wars, ethnic slaughters, political intrigue, and social upheavals. Even the earth itself, under the governorship of Satan, had crumbled into dangerous disrepair. Famines, pestilences, disease, and an endless list of calamities plagued humankind relentlessly.

Instead of identifying the correct source of the problems—as the Creator had done when He pointed out Satan's starring role in the deception of Adam and Eve—many Old Testament writers repeatedly included statements such as, "And the Lord brought forth [insert any number of catastrophes: failed crops, pestilence, plagues, destruction, and death]." Satan had cunningly made sure that God was blamed for every misfortune. The truth—the real reason for calamities—had been lost for generations.

I once asked a man whose opinion I respect for his thoughts about why God was blamed for such ungodly behavior during those centuries. His answer stunned me with its simplicity and, I believe, absolute correctness. He said that in the Old Testament things were often attributed to God that He didn't *stop*. Interesting!

So, what exactly does God have in mind for us? Consider this revealing text: " 'For I know the plans I have for you,' declares the Lord, 'plans to prosper you and not to harm you, plans to give you hope and a future' " (Jeremiah 29:11).

Now *that's* the kind of God I want to worship. *That's* the kind of God I want on my team.

Out there in the wild, before you lay blame for something bad that happens to you, stop and think: *Is this the way God acts? Or is this the way people* say *God acts?* In our messed up world, those two concepts can get very confused. It's important that we know the truth.

* * * * *

Most Important Work

"Glory to God in the highest heaven,
and on earth peace to those on whom his favor rests."

—Luke 2:14

So, what had happened to our tender, loving God, the Father represented by the Creator as He strolled with Adam and Eve in the cool of the evening, who made singing birds and splashing fish and provided a safe haven for all living creatures?

Throughout the Old Testament, we hear of God the Father slaughtering entire armies, drowning almost everyone in a worldwide flood, smiting the firstborn of Egypt, ordering the destruction of whole villages (including women and children), and striking down anyone who would dare go against His word. That perfect, peace-loving Being had been transformed into a violent, fearful, bloodthirsty tyrant.

Or was something else at play here? More to the point, was *someone* else calling the shots, laying the blame, turning the hearts of human beings away from God? Was Satan the serpent continuing the crusade of lies and deceit he'd launched in Eden? In my opinion, yes!

This brings me back to that lonely hillside outside of Bethlehem. Two thousand years ago, something amazing happened there. God—the tender, loving Being who for so long had served as a scapegoat for humankind's violent tendencies, need for revenge, and endless desire for self-promotion—sent His Son, Jesus, to be born as a certified flesh-and-blood human being.

There was no one there to welcome Him except a group of lowly shepherds who, while watching their flocks by night, learned that the world as they knew it was about to change forever. Over that field, a host of angels announced that, after a long separation, God and humans were about to be reunited.

In just a few short years, those terrible misconceptions and misrepresentations of who God is and how God acts would be addressed in some profound ways. Christ's most important work would be revealing the truth about His Father's character and reestablishing something long lost: a personal connection between God and humankind. That was the central theme of plan B.

PART 2

Who Is GOD REALLY?

Spoiler alert:
He's not who Satan says He is.

Man of Mystery

So, here we are, four thousand years from Creation, and something incredible has happened on Earth. God has become a total mystery.

Oh, there's no question that He, or something like Him, exists. People worship all types of gods. You can see representations of them everywhere—in homes, places of business, government buildings, temples, shrines, and even carefully selected items from nature. People bow down, bring offerings, pray, scream, cut themselves, have sex, plead, and murder their children and each other in an endless effort to appease their gods. They blame, confess, humiliate, and otherwise desecrate themselves in the name of their chosen deity.

Sound familiar? Wouldn't it be fair to say that, in today's world, God remains a mystery?

I've circled the globe, living in a wide variety of cultures, and have seen it with my own eyes. People will go to incredible lengths in an all-out attempt to catch the attention or gain the favor of their god. Not a lot has changed since Satan convinced humanity that God really couldn't be known, trusted, or loved. The best you can do—according to the devil—is be afraid of Him.

The question remains: Who is God really? What's He like? How does He act? More to the point, if God stood before me, face-to-face, what would He think of *me*? Would I receive a welcoming hug or a judgmental shove?

When Jesus packed His travel bags, laced up His sandals, kissed His mom goodbye, and headed south from Nazareth toward the Jordan River in search of John the Baptist, He was doing more than starting His official ministry on Earth. He was on a mission to reveal something that had been lost for millennia.

While some Old Testament writers reflected on God's "softer side"—David, for instance, often wrote of His majesty and grace—by and large, it was His wrath and displeasure that filled the minds of followers and the pages of Holy Writ. Now, three decades after the angels sang over Bethlehem, it was time to set the record straight. It was time for God to reintroduce God to the world. But it wouldn't be easy.

* * * * *

Blessings and Curses

The Jewish religion of Christ's day—a natural outgrowth of what people thought God demanded of them—was a boiling cauldron of dos and don'ts, of sacrifices and festivals, of stringent rules and hairsplitting regulations. Every aspect of life carried a spiritual meaning, complete with a religious ceremony or requirement tightly attached to it.

Anything good that happened to you was labeled a blessing from God. Anything bad that happened to you was considered a curse from God. The only way you could stay in sync with the Divine was to do the right things, at the right times, and in the right ways.

Which begs the question, Where was Satan in all of this? Why weren't fingers pointing in his direction whenever bad things happened? Even sickness, the cornerstone of evil, was laid at God's feet. As often happens today, illness was considered an indicator of Heaven's displeasure with a person's choices.

One day, Jesus and His disciples came upon a man who had been blind since birth. The disciples asked, "Rabbi, who sinned, this man or his parents, that he was born blind?" (John 9:2). The possibility that the poor gentleman was sightless because of accident, disease, or some other misfortune didn't even cross their minds.

Into this mixed-up, confused, and utterly disillusioned world, Jesus stepped. He was not only determined to save souls from the grasp of Satan—who He knew full well was the source of *all* suffering and sin—but also equally determined to save souls from the firm grasp of the distorted belief systems of that day.

That distortion continues. How important it is that in the wild, you and I fully understand and appreciate the true character of God. It can save us a boatload of heartache and fear. Heaven knows that this life contains enough of those already.

* * * * *

Wrath of God

Are you ready for a little deep thinking? Turn off your cell phone, switch off your PlayStation for a moment, and stay with me, because this is very important for us all to understand.

One word that seems to be a favorite in the Old Testament when it comes to God is *wrath*. His wrath seems to spread like a blanket of doom and gloom over everyone and everything. Time and time again, it seemed God was saying, "I'm upset. I'm angry. You have so disappointed Me that it leaves Me no choice but to bring terrible suffering down on you. Or I may choose to kill you." Try to get that someone special to love and respect you using that pitch!

Consider this prime example from the Old Testament. Warning of the destruction of Jerusalem at the hands of the Babylonians, God, through the prophet Ezekiel, states,

> "Because I tried to cleanse you but you would not be cleansed from your impurity, you will not be clean again until my wrath against you has subsided.
>
> "I the LORD have spoken. The time has come for me to act. I will not hold back; I will not have pity, nor will I relent. You will be judged according to your conduct and your actions, declares the Sovereign LORD" (Ezekiel 24:13, 14).

Yikes! Sure enough, Jerusalem fell amid horrific destruction and loss of life.

The question no one seemed to ask is, Did God use His power to destroy those at whom these words were directed, or did their rebellion against Him separate them from His protection, leading to their destruction?

Truth is, the children of Israel had turned their backs on God—just as Adam and Eve had. They'd rejected His methods and principles outright—just as Adam and Eve had. God, in His love, gave that nation exactly what they'd chosen for themselves: a life *without* Him. Then along came the Babylonians, and the rest is history.

Centuries earlier, God had sounded this alarm:

> "For a fire will be kindled by my wrath,
> one that burns down to the realm of the dead below.
> It will devour the earth and its harvests
> and set afire the foundations of the mountains.
>
> "I will heap calamities on them
> and spend my arrows against them.
> I will send wasting famine against them,
> consuming pestilence and deadly plague;
> I will send against them the fangs of wild beasts,
> the venom of vipers that glide in the dust" (Deuteronomy 32:22–24).

The dire warning goes on and on and on.

Then, hidden within this rant, comes a peek into the true character of God. No one seemed to notice these words that explained the *real* reason for the coming disasters and how a weaker enemy could overpower an entire nation:

> If only they were wise and would understand this
> and discern what their end will be!
> How could one man chase a thousand,
> or two put ten thousand to flight,
> unless their Rock had sold them,
> unless the LORD had given them up? (verses 29, 30).

"*Given them up.*" There it is! God's wrath isn't an act of destruction. It's an act of letting go. Destruction is what happens when God *withdraws* His protective presence.

What many consider punishment is simply the result of living outside of God's defending power. So, if you ever find yourself in this type of sad situation in the wild, don't feel punished by what happens. Instead, feel alone. Then do something about it. Reconnect with God through prayer and Bible study. He's still there, knocking at your heart's door.

* * * * *

The Father of All Lies Strikes Again

I find it very interesting—and heartbreaking—that the devil has convinced most Christians that the final and everlasting destruction of sin and sinners (commonly called hell) is brought about by the hand of God. Such a belief is the ultimate slap in the face. The natural result of sin—its own implosion or self-destruction—is considered a judgment-driven act performed by God Himself. But, as we learned in Eden, God's sole purpose was *and is* to create and sustain life. Yup, we've come so far from the Garden!

What about you? Out here in the wild, do you ever feel that the bad stuff that happens to you is the result of God's unhappiness concerning your actions, thoughts, or plans?

As I remember, the teenage mind is a very active place, filled with endless ideas and desires. (By the way, that doesn't change with age—you just learn to be more focused, that's all.) As a teenager, you want to change the world, but you're not sure how to go about doing it. So, you try this or try that, and sometimes it works, and sometimes it's a disaster. You may tend to think that what works is God's leading and what doesn't work is God slapping your hand because you were dumb enough to consider such a crazy idea. You beat yourself up so that God doesn't have to.

Well, think again, my friend. This world is filled with good people who fail and bad people who succeed mightily. God isn't God only to those who find success. He's God to those of us who fail (and fail again), who sin, who act un-Christlike, who get lost along the way. Don't ever judge yourself by outcomes. Judge yourself by what happened on the cross.

The Son of God knew what He had to do. He had to overcome four thousand years of Satan's lies and humans' misunderstanding of who and what God is. Jesus had to open the door to the possibility that God is an agent of love, not wrath. Christ would accomplish this by becoming a living, breathing, visual representation of the truth—a mission that would cost Him His life.

* * * * *

Ultimate Good Meets Ultimate Evil

After His baptism in the Jordan River at the hands of His cousin, John the Baptist, Christ "was led by the Spirit into the wilderness, where for forty days he was tempted by the devil" (Luke 4:1, 2).

I find it important that Jesus gave Satan first crack at Him. Not church leaders. Not the Romans. Not some spiritual guru sitting on a mountaintop somewhere. No, He chose to meet evil face-to-face at its very source. This event took place even before Jesus had any type of human support structure surrounding Him. No disciples. No followers. No cheering section. Just Christ, the serpent, and the barren desert.

By the way, *barren* is a kind word for that area. I've stood among those mountains listening to the wind whistle through bone-dry canyons. There's nothing there to inspire or protect you. Words like *desolate*, *wild*, *bleak*, and *depressing* spring to mind. It's not a place where you'd want to meet a friend, much less the most dangerous enemy on earth. The desert beyond Jordan even boasts a sea called Dead.

Then there's this: Jesus "ate nothing during those days, and at the end of them he was hungry" (verse 2).

Christ stripped Himself of *all* comforts and security. His second earthly confrontation with the evil one (the first was in the Garden of Eden) would be completely on Satan's terms. All Christ had in His corner—all He ever had—was His Father.

When we examine what happened, we begin to realize that this showdown between good and evil was for *our* benefit. It presents us with a vivid description of how we as Christians should confront evil in our own lives.

My friend, don't ever feel powerless out there in the wild. Don't ever think you're alone. You're not. You have a Father too.

* * * * *

If

Weak from hunger, friendless, and alone, Jesus stands nose-to-nose with the ancient enemy. Satan's first double-edged attack hits Christ right where He's most vulnerable. He says, "If you are the Son of God, tell this stone to become bread" (Luke 4:3).

"*If* you are the Son of God"?

It's the same line Satan often uses on us in the wild. "*If* you were a Christian, you wouldn't be acting like this, be thinking what you're thinking, or having the problems you're having. *If* you were a Christian, you'd know the answers to life's most troubling questions and be happy. You could heal yourself or dig yourself out of the pit you've fallen into." The evil one often reserves these types of attacks for moments when we're most vulnerable . . . when we're angry, disappointed, grieving, or hungry for love.

Ignoring the doubt Satan threw in His face, Jesus answered, "It is written: 'Man shall not live on bread alone' " (verse 4).

Here, I think Christ is saying, "There's more to life than what we think we need. I, along with those who choose to walk with Me, are not immune to hunger, doubt, or sadness. We feel fear, uncertainty, and disappointment. The difference is that we know there's more. Much more."

Thanks to Christ's response, when I experience such feelings, I understand they don't signal the unhappiness of my heavenly Father. They simply indicate that I'm a human being living in a confused and frustrating world of sin and, at times, experiencing the impact of my own wrong choices and the crushing load of guilt placed on me by generations of evil.

I find great comfort in that thought. Doubt isn't a God thing. It's a devil thing. When I feel uncertain about my relationship with my Creator—when I feel that my life is out of control—I know there's a God who's watching over me in love, not judging me in anger. Even while I'm reaping the painful rewards of my sins, He's waiting to show me that there's more. Much more. I need to shift my attention from what I think I need to what He freely offers.

Later, talking to a crowd of people on the shores of the Sea of Galilee, Christ identified the bread for which we all should hunger. He told them, "I am the bread of life. Whoever comes to me will never go hungry" (John 6:35).

Satan was tempting Christ with earthly food just as he tempts us with earthly enticements that satisfy our often-perverted appetites. In His response to the evil one, Jesus reminded us that we should hunger for the greater food—the sustenance of salvation offered only through Him.

* * * * *

Authority and Splendor

When his first attempt failed, "the devil led him [Jesus] up to a high place and showed him in an instant all the kingdoms of the world. And he said to him, 'I will give you all their authority and splendor; it has been given to me, and I can give it to anyone I want to. If you worship me, it will all be yours' " (Luke 4:5–7).

That's like a prisoner saying he owns the prison because he's been forced to live there.

Jesus didn't dignify Satan's lie with a snarky comeback. His answer was in the form of a reminder, perhaps urging His tempter to consider why he ended up on Earth in the first place. In response, Jesus said, "It is written: 'Worship the Lord your God and serve him only' " (verse 8).

We as human beings must come to the place where we fully understand that much of what we hear in the wild is a lie, that truth was—and still is—the first victim of sin. It's not that the people who tell those lies know they're doing it. They're simply reaching conclusions and making choices using principles and ideas that are created by Satan but aren't in keeping with God's ideal.

Reflecting on my years of promoting health and well-being, I know that these lies can draw us into a life of sickness and pain. We hear such falsehoods all the time. "Animal products are safe and nutritious to eat. They do a body good." Or, "Take this, go there, watch that, listen to those voices, fill your mind with stimulating images, burn the midnight oil, strive to be a one-percenter, skip the weekly day of rest, live the good life, nothing matters but what matters to you." The list goes on and on and on—every item a direct outgrowth of Satan's original falsehood, "You will not surely die."

Somewhere in that noise, somewhere in that avalanche of fibs, we need to hear Jesus saying, "Worship the Lord your God and serve Him only."

You and I need to realize that God knows exactly where we are and what we're going through. He's seen the enticements and heard the siren call of earthly power. Satan made sure that his little PowerPoint presentation included all the top-drawer stuff. But Jesus didn't fall for it because He knew what was really important in this land of lies. It's whom we worship. It's to whom we give our allegiance.

Money, fame, power—all perfectly fine rewards for hard work—are no substitute for a personal and ongoing reverence for God. We lose sight of that fact at our peril.

* * * * *

High Above the Temple

Finally, the devil took Jesus on a virtual tour of the Jewish capital city, Jerusalem. Together they stood on the highest point of the temple. Below them spread Solomon's grand design filled with worshipers and architectural wonders.

Satan then offered an invitation.

> "If you are the Son of God," he said, "throw yourself down from here. For it is written:
>
> " 'He will command his angels concerning you
> to guard you carefully;
> they will lift you up in their hands,
> so that you will not strike your foot against a stone' " (Luke 4:9–11).

Are you surprised that the devil quoted Scripture? In this encounter, Satan demonstrates that he knows the Bible well, but he also shows that he interprets it to fit his purposes.

Satan's temptation was a powerful one. If Jesus refuted those words or refused to comply with Satan's suggestion, He'd be calling into question the very validity of the Old Testament Bible—the cornerstone of the Jewish religion.

How many of us have faced a similar temptation? How many of us have stepped out in what we call faith when, in reality, we're using faith as a cover for our ambitions?

Faith, by definition, isn't necessarily something that supports our desires. Instead, it's an emotional motivation that allows us to act on deeply held beliefs. Stepping out in faith should result from careful preparation, not an act of blind presumption.

Satan wants us to believe that God's watchful eye and helpful hand are surrounding us at all times. But, here's the rub. What if we've rejected God? What if we've told our heavenly Father, "Thanks, but no thanks. Just let me live my life on my terms"? What happens then?

That might be a good question to ask those who refused to build or board the ark in Noah's day. Like them, sometimes we want it both ways. We want to laugh at God, reject His ideals, and walk all over His commandments. And then, when we're reaping the terrible rewards of our folly, we want to look to God to save us because "He will command his angels concerning you to guard you carefully" (verse 10).

I see it all the time. Someone wholeheartedly rejects God's original health plan (the Eden ideal of a whole-food, plant-exclusive diet mixed with fresh air, sunshine, clean water, and honest work—more on this later). This person spends his or her life eating destructive, highly refined foods and living a debilitating lifestyle filled with little sleep, high stress, and anger and then ends up with heart disease, type 2 diabetes, cancer, obesity, or the beginning stages of Alzheimer's. "Heal me!" he or she prays. "Remember, God, You promised!"

God, whose ability to love goes far beyond mine, does what He can with what's left. But, at this point, we really shouldn't expect God to erase fifty or sixty years of health rebellion and make everything all well again. We do reap what we—and the generations who came before us—sow. Can you say, "Genetics"?

Out here in the wild, we really need to come to grips with that fact and not blame God when everything goes south. How much better it is to set our feet firmly on faith early and then enjoy the journey and the amazing spiritual, mental, and physical benefits it offers along the way as we keep to the original script God wrote in Eden.

* * * * *

The Test

How did Jesus answer this third and final temptation of the devil to put God to the test as they were perched on the high pinnacle of the temple in Jerusalem? He said simply, "Do not put the Lord your God to the test" (Luke 4:12).

I've discovered here in the wild that the answers to my prayers and the miracles I want to happen in my life don't just fall from the sky. They usually come slowly, over time, as I educate myself and get to know the real God who's waiting in Scripture.

Healing for my body doesn't arrive in the form of a magic pill. It comes as I begin to understand and implement God's original health plan as outlined during Creation week.

Healing for my mind takes place as I contemplate the truth as God presents it, not spending time in frustration over Satan's falsehoods.

Healing for my spirit is the underlying result of worshiping the God of heaven, not the god of some earthly religion. With this renewed understanding of how God works, we don't have to put Him to the test because His ways have become our ways, His thoughts our thoughts, His desires our desires. Like David, we can say, "I desire to do your will, my God; your law is within my heart" (Psalm 40:8).

That day in the desert, Jesus pulled back the curtain of Satan's lies and confusion even further, revealing a God who offers much more than this sinful world can ever offer. He provides a safe and secure place for worship and outlines the very best way for each of us to live within His laws of love. Behind the obscuring curtain, we find no wrath, no vengeance, no anger, no fire and brimstone, and no rejection. Instead, we discover a God of love, acceptance, and forgiveness.

But Christ had only begun His work of revealing the true character of God to the world. What lay ahead would push His resolve and His mission to the absolute breaking point.

* * * * *

Eyewitnesses

For thirty-three years, the Son of God lived among us—eating our food, walking our roads, and shivering from the same winter winds that chill us. There were eyewitnesses to His life and times—people who later told stories about Him, wrote about Him, and were stunned by the life-altering power of His unique message. For one shining moment, God stood in plain view, illuminated by His own light and expressed by His own words.

It's here in the shadows of Jesus' life that we hear God's unfiltered voice and see His loving hands in action. Here we also find the answers to the nagging questions many people ask: What must I do to be saved? Who will serve as my judge? Who will decide whether I'm a worthy candidate for heaven?

If we stand before the Old Testament God, our outlook can appear dim at times. We're all sinners, broken vessels, imperfect illustrations of what a Christian should be. We get angry and experience doubt. We put ourselves before others far too often. We occasionally stumble along, not even knowing—or caring—about anything spiritual. What is God to do with someone like you or me?

The answer comes suddenly in Scripture. Christ, talking with His disciples on the eve of His capture and crucifixion, stated, "If anyone hears my words but does not keep them, I do not judge that person. For I did not come to judge the world, but to save the world" (John 12:47).

This is good news for those of us in the wild. God isn't our judge—He's our Savior! We can feel safe and secure in His hands. No fear, no uncertainty, no doubt. What a beautiful way to live!

* * * * *

Words, Words, Words

If God doesn't judge us, then who does? Consider this astonishing insight from Christ Himself: "There is a judge for the one who rejects me and does not accept my words; the very words I have spoken will condemn them at the last day" (John 12:48). Wait a minute. I'm condemned by words? How does *that* work?

Someone says to me, "Charles, if you climb to the top of that cliff and jump off, you're going to fall to the rocks below and die." So, with that warning ringing in my ears, I climb to the top of the cliff and jump. Sure enough, I fall to the rocks and die. What killed me? What pronounced judgment on me? The person who delivered the warning? No. My life ended because I ignored the words.

According to the unfiltered, uncensored Jesus of the New Testament Gospels, judgment rides on our acceptance or rejection of God's warning message. What happens to us on that final "judgment" day isn't an act of a wrathful God. We choose whether to jump off the cliff—or not. We choose which path we set our course on and, in doing so, accept the destination determined by that path.

Just to be sure, does this amazing proclamation apply to God the Father as well as His Son? Jesus continues, "For I did not speak on my own, but the Father who sent me commanded me to say all that I have spoken. I know that his command leads to eternal life" (John 12:49, 50). While some of God's words may serve to condemn us, others serve to save us! Jesus seems to be saying, "Don't give up. There are *other* words you need to hear—words directly from your heavenly Father!"

There's salvation riding on the wings of God's words as spoken by His Son. There's hope hidden in every syllable.

* * * * *

Walk the Talk

Did Jesus demonstrate those saving, nonjudgmental words He spoke?* Did He put them into action?

Three times—as recorded in Scripture—Christ came face-to-face with known sinners. Three times He had the opportunity to judge them openly and severely. Three times He illustrated with His actions the part He and our heavenly Father long to play in our lives.

Anytime someone tries to tell you that God is a stern, wrathful judge bringing condemnation down on wayward sinners, remember these stories.

The first had to do with a big tree and a little man.

Like the children's Bible song says, "Zacchaeus was a wee little man."† He was small both in stature and in character. As the chief tax collector, he went around forcing his fellow countrymen to pay taxes to the despised Romans who occupied the Israelites' land. He often collected more than necessary, making himself very wealthy. Is it any wonder that the Jewish people despised him?

One day, as recorded in Luke 19, Zacchaeus was in Jericho doing what he did best when he heard that Jesus, the famous Rabbi who healed the sick, was passing through. Taxman Zacchaeus decided he wanted to see this popular Stranger. But, being a *wee* little man, standing in a curious crowd afforded him a perfect view of a lot of backs and bellies.

Never letting his lack of height interfere with his tall plans, he looked around for a solution and found it towering nearby. Sycamore fig trees dotted the landscape, and just down the road stood a wonderful specimen, complete with sturdy branches and enough leaves to hide his curiosity.

Then along came Jesus, surrounded by attentive disciples, a group of recently healed sick people, a gaggle of questioning admirers, and even a few hecklers. Zacchaeus smirked inwardly. He'd found the best seat in the house for the spectacle unfolding below him.

Reaching the tree, Jesus suddenly stopped.

I hold my breath at this point in the story. *Now Zacchaeus is going to get it,* I think to myself. *That little thief has come face-to-face with the God of the*

---

* Portions of this section and the following have been previously published as Charles Mills, "Mission Fulfilled," *Pacific Union Recorder*, October 2021, https://issuu.com/pacificunionrecorder/docs/1021recorder/s/13596774; Charles Mills, "Judgment of Love," *Signs of the Times*, October 2011, https://www.signstimes.com/?p=article&a=44142430201.786; Charles Mills, "How Jesus Treated Bad People," Hope This Way, accessed April 25, 2022, https://www.hopethisway.org/how-jesus-treated-bad-people/.

† Author unknown.

universe—the mighty Judge. Stand back, everyone!

Instead, with a smile spreading across His rugged, suntanned face, Jesus looked up—right at Zacchaeus. The taxman grinned self-consciously. "Hello," he called down, suddenly wishing he were much smaller than he already was.

"Zacchaeus," the Rabbi called, "come down immediately. I must stay at your house today" (Luke 19:5).

In stunned wonder, the short man made the long journey from his tree limb to the ground. "You want to come to *my* house?" he asked.

Christ nodded.

"Well . . . this way," Zacchaeus stammered as he pointed down the road. "Just . . . follow me."

Later, after Zacchaeus and Jesus had spent time together, an incredible thing happened to the little man. He grew up—not in height, but in character. "Look, Lord!" he announced. "Here and now I give half of my possessions to the poor, and if I have cheated anybody out of anything, I will pay back four times the amount" (verse 8).

Zacchaeus, the crooked tax collector, had met Jesus, the Judge, face-to-face. His sentence? "Invite Me to your home for dinner."

* * * * *

Undercover Sinner

One day, just after dawn, Jesus was spending some quiet time at the temple in Jerusalem when a group of men showed up and unceremoniously tossed a woman at His feet. "Teacher," they said, "this woman was caught in the act of adultery. In the Law Moses commanded us to stone such women. Now what do you say?" (John 8:4, 5).

Yes, Jesus, I think to myself, *what* do You *say? She's a harlot, a home-wrecker, an unrepentant sinner.*

Silently, Jesus bent down and started writing in the sand with His finger. I have no idea what He wrote, but the men saw something there that made them decide that they were late for important appointments elsewhere.

Soon, only Jesus and the accused remained—sinner and Savior standing face-to-face. "Woman . . . ," He said quietly, "has no one condemned you?" (verse 10).

The woman, sensing that this confrontation was turning out quite differently than she had expected, answered in a whisper, "No one, sir" (verse 11).

The next words out of Jesus' mouth, combined with the story of Zacchaeus, should change forever the way we look at God's judgment here in the wild.

Gazing intently into the eyes of a woman caught in adultery, Jesus said, "Then neither do I condemn you. . . . Go now and leave your life of sin" (verse 11).

Judgment day for that woman had arrived on the wings of forgiveness and an invitation to live a better, happier life. That's good news for all of us sinners.

* * * * *

Hanging in the Balance

Finally, we arrive at a very dark place—a hilltop just outside the walls of Jerusalem, where we find Christ hanging in agony from a Roman cross. On either side of Him, each nailed to his own cross, is a sinner. These two thieves' lives had been filled with violence and lawlessness.

One cursed the dying Savior with these mocking words: "Aren't you the Messiah? Save yourself and us!" (Luke 23:39).

The other thief turned to his fellow criminal and groaned through his pain. " 'Don't you fear God,' he said, 'since you are under the same sentence? We are punished justly, for we are getting what our deeds deserve. But this man has done nothing wrong' " (verses 40, 41).

Then, looking over at the Savior, he said, "Jesus, remember me when you come into your kingdom" (verse 42).

Jesus answered, "Truly I tell you, today you will be with me in paradise" (verse 43).

Both thieves suffered and died that day. But only one felt the impact of divine judgment before passing away. No, it wasn't the cursing thief. He died without hope. That was his choice. It was the one who made a simple request from his dying heart: "Remember me." At that moment, he changed his future. At that moment, he chose an entirely different outcome—eternal life with Jesus in heaven.

It's not God we need to fear when it comes to our judgment. It's not His wrath or His vengeance that will prove to be our undoing. What will happen to us is directly connected to our relationship to His words, His laws, and His guidance. They set the standard on the road of life as we journey through the wild. They provide the guardrail and point the way. God's words also warn of those things that *we will bring upon ourselves* if we choose another path. Sin imprisons. Sin destroys. Love provides the only escape.

* * * * *

The Prodigal

The true, life-changing concept of God's judgment also shines brightly in a story centered on a father, a son, and a herd of pigs.

The fifteenth chapter of Luke could very well be called the "lost chapter." In it, we find the parables of the lost sheep, the lost coin, and the lost son. The story of the lost son caught my attention one day and provided an important insight. The words belong to Jesus. The story belongs to us.

"There was a man who had two sons. The younger one said to his father, 'Father, give me my share of the estate.' So he divided his property between them" (verses 11, 12).

Nothing unusual here. Both sons got their inheritance. Both enjoyed their share of their father's fortune.

"Not long after that, the younger son got together all he had, set off for a distant country and there squandered his wealth in wild living" (verse 13). Again, that was his choice. After all, it was his money.

But then a famine hit, and the whole country suffered, including the now penniless son. He found a job feeding a herd of pigs. "He longed to fill his stomach with the pods that the pigs were eating, but no one gave him anything" (verse 16).

Then Jesus told His listeners, "When he [the son] came to his senses, he said, 'How many of my father's hired servants have food to spare, and here I am starving to death! I will set out and go back to my father and say to him: Father, I have sinned against heaven and against you. I am no longer worthy to be called your son; make me like one of your hired servants.' So he got up and went to his father" (verses 17–20).

I can imagine Jesus leaning forward slightly as He spoke the next words. He wanted His hearers to understand clearly what their experience could be if they chose to make some changes in their lives and return to their heavenly Father.

"But while he [the son] was still a long way off, his father saw him and was filled with compassion for him; he ran to his son, threw his arms around him and kissed him" (verse 20). Dad wouldn't even listen to the son's well-rehearsed "I Was a Fool" speech. Instead, a great feast was prepared. "He was lost," the father proclaimed to anyone who would listen, "and is found" (verse 32).

Did you notice some important points in this story? First, the son left the father. The father didn't leave the son. But the father did do something. He let him go.

Second, after the son had squandered his inheritance, he experienced the consequences of his actions. His suffering was of his own making. Dad wasn't even there! Dad had no part in the "judgment" that brought the son to his knees.

Third, when the son decided to return home, the father—the one who had been rejected, the one who had freely given away part of his treasure only for it to be squandered, the one who had every right to condemn the boy's actions—ran to meet the returning child, wrapped his arms around him, and planted kisses of joy all over his young face.

We must never consider God anything less than a hopeful Father eagerly waiting for our return, searching the horizon, trying to catch a glimpse of our tired, stumbling form after we've come to our senses. To consider Him anything less is a misrepresentation of His character and a humanizing of His purposes. A God of love can do nothing but accept us back into His arms if we're willing to make the journey. If we're not, we perish by our own hands—not His.

Someday, I plan to stand beside the taxman, the woman, the thief, and all my fellow prodigals and look into the face of the One whose words not only provided the warning but also established a way of escape from sin.

After we leave the wild, we'll walk streets of gold because we chose to believe and trust our heavenly Father—the Divine Being revealed by Jesus. No longer will we see Him "through a glass, darkly," as the Bible says in 1 Corinthians 13:12 (KJV). We'll know who He really is because we've spent time in His presence, prayerfully listening to and learning to follow His words. We'll see Him face-to-face and spend eternity experiencing the gentle, life-affirming touch of His judgment of love.

PART 3

WITNESS *to the* WORLD

How to share your faith—without looking or sounding weird!

Confession

I have a confession to make. I'm a preacher's kid (PK). Not only that, but I'm also a missionary's kid (MK). My father was an ordained minister of the Seventh-day Adventist Church and served in mission posts overseas in Korea (where I was born), Japan, the Philippines, Singapore, and Lebanon. During my college years, I spent a year in Japan as a student missionary, teaching conversational English to young professionals in Osaka.

So, you can safely say that the missionary mindset drives me. I grew up thinking that service to others is the highest calling for any Christian. I still think that today. That's why I'm sitting at my computer right now doing my best to communicate with you the important topics of understanding who God is and learning how to live the Christian life out in the wild. It's my way of serving you, my young reader. Right now, *you* are the focus of my career, my witness, and my spiritual passion.

Being a PK or MK gives you a certain perspective. The whole world is your mission field. To serve people who may not look, sound, or act like you is why you exist. It's for them that you put the talents and skills you possess into action. It's not about you. It's *never* about you. It's about others. Period.

I've discovered that I experience the most doubt and uncertainty when I turn my focus inward. That's when I begin to question my place in this world and whether I'm up to the task of sharing God's love with others. Sometimes I feel downright unworthy and vulnerable. But when I put my head down and motor on, using what I know and what I can do to make it through the day while focusing on the needs of others, something amazing happens. First, I make it through the day! Second, at the end of the day or week or month, I look back and am shocked at what the Lord was able to accomplish through me. While I was hard at work, He was blessing others through my work in ways I couldn't even see.

That's the formula: I work. God blesses. It's a powerful combination you can enjoy as well.

And that brings me to another confession. I'm not trying to change your life with this book, and there's a good reason for that. I can't. All I can do is put words together that hopefully make sense to you and keep you coming back to read a few more pages from time to time. However, if your heart is moved in any way as you read or think about what's written here—if you reach new conclusions and find yourself being drawn closer to Jesus—*that's not because of me*. That's because the Holy Spirit is at work in your heart. Pretty impressive, huh?

When it comes to your witness to the world, I just identified the two most important elements: (1) serving others must be your goal, and (2) success isn't about you—it's about the Holy Spirit.

So, my friend, are you ready to learn how to share your faith without looking or sounding totally weird? Let's do this!

* * * * *

The Crying Man

I want to tell you a story.

Morning rush-hour drivers vied for position along the tangled maze of streets crisscrossing Silver Spring, Maryland. Already, the temperature hovered around the ninety-degree mark. It was going to be another hot, humid day in the city.

Tempers burned and horns blared as accountants, secretaries, bank presidents, and computer programmers inched toward downtown destinations, trying to ignore the brown haze that hung over the streets like acid fog and taxed air conditioners and lungs alike. So much work. So little time.

I took my place in the line of cars waiting to turn left onto Fenton Street, my mind running through a seemingly endless checklist of things to do that day. There were people depending on me, budget battles to wage, and projects to bring back on schedule.

That's when I saw him, a man in an expensive three-piece suit standing on the corner, face buried in his hands. His broad shoulders sagged as his body swayed back and forth. Tousled brown hair flowed over his fingers as tiny drops of moisture squeezed through and fell silently to the sidewalk.

No one noticed. No one stopped. The crying man stood there alone in a sea of humanity.

He looked like a little boy lost. I glanced about, half expecting to see a kind-faced mother rush to his side and gather him up in her arms. The crying man would look into her comforting eyes and tell her of the pain ravaging his heart. But no one came.

Cars eased past or idled impatiently by the curb, their drivers and passengers lost in their own sorrows.

I stared at the scene for a long moment, moved by the passion of his distress. My arms ached to hold the man, to speak encouragement to him, to tell him that everything would be all right. But we were separated by traffic, by time, and by expectations of privacy.

The sudden angry blast of a horn drew my attention to the light as it changed from red to green. I pressed on the accelerator and eased around the corner. I watched the crying man grow smaller and smaller in the rearview mirror. Then he was gone, swallowed up by the swirling mix of faces and vehicles, vanishing completely in the cold press of humanity and the awful reality of modern life. I would never see him again. He would never know that I witnessed his tears, that I cared, that I loved him.

"Oh, Lord," I prayed through tears of my own, "comfort the crying man. Forgive my life so filled with deadlines and responsibilities. Forgive me for letting the expectations of others keep me from acting on Your impulse. Bring me another crying man. Please. Give me another chance."

I looked around at the faces rushing by. But this time, I was searching.

That day, I was taught a silent and valuable lesson. I found that I cared for the crying man because I felt his pain. Like him, I've cried while surrounded by an indifferent sea of humanity. I've had life hit me so hard that I allowed feelings of frustration and sorrow to overwhelm me. I knew exactly how that man felt. We both needed the same thing. We both needed God in our lives. That was *me* on the street corner!

From that moment on, I knew that nothing would stand in the way of my witness. I would boldly proclaim my admiration for God with anyone, anywhere, anytime—because I knew what *I* needed to hear.

Being a witness requires your presence where it's needed most. Don't live your life gazing at your own reflection. Look around. Notice the needs. Search for ways to be of service.

* * * * *

Speeding Ticket

I'm about to share with you one of my strangest witnesses *ever*. It seems that opportunities to share God's love are all around you . . . even, sometimes, behind you with a flashing light. This experience happened soon after I graduated from college.

Traffic on the 405 freeway wasn't heavy yet as I turned my motorcycle north and sprinted toward the Grapevine. I was leaving the smog-tainted atmosphere of Los Angeles for a weekend in sweet-smelling Yosemite National Park, my favorite destination on earth.

As I was passing Van Nuys, I noticed an all-too-familiar sight in my rearview mirror. Apparently, one of Los Angeles County's finest thought my rate of escape from the San Fernando Valley was a little too eager and wanted to spend some quality time with me.

"Where do you work?" the officer asked, making notations on his clipboard. I explained that I was a member of a film crew that produced Christ-centered television programs. His pen paused mid-word. "I don't believe in religion," he said, and then he finished his scribbling and handed me a ticket. "How could God allow such suffering in the world?"

Feeling suddenly evangelistic, I responded, "What would you say if I told you that I wasn't going to pay this?" I held the paper up in front of him.

"Hey, you were speeding," he warned. "You gotta pay. That's the law."

"Then why should sinners who ignore God's protective laws, turn their backs on His warnings, and even curse His name get off the hook?" I asked. "We bring most suffering on ourselves. We do the crime. We gotta do the time. I could've slowed down a little and not earned this ticket. All that was required was relaxing the wrist of my right hand. Should I now blame you because I have to cough up hard-earned money to pay for my error in judgment? Are you the bad guy here? Is this all your fault? Should I now hate you because I ended up with this invitation to support the county's law-enforcement efforts?"

My uniformed friend didn't answer. He just stood by my motorcycle, shaking his head slowly, letting the simple truth of God's law sink into his mind, allowing its timeless message to slip past years of excuses and anger, past the doubt and self-pity, past the ingrained traditional image of our heavenly Father. For the next hour, we tarried by the center divider, the cop and the lawbreaker, discussing God and humanity, comparing our small encounter with the vast cosmic struggle going on between good and evil. The parallels were undeniable, the lessons to be learned so real and tangible to us both.

In our little drama, surrounded by the rumble of cars and trucks, he'd become a god of sorts, defending his law against someone who had, for a moment, chosen to ignore it. I'd become the sinner, defiantly insisting that I knew best and could drive at any speed that fitted my desire to escape for the weekend. The ticket I held in my hand reminded me that a law existed. If I'd stopped and been totally honest about the matter, the whole system made perfect sense. Speed kills. Laws save lives and bottom lines, including mine.

Before we parted company, the policeman said he'd think about what we'd discussed. Later, as I paid the ticket, so did I.

* * * * *

Show, Don't Tell

There's an old adage that writers often hear. "Don't tell your readers what a character is doing," we're instructed in countless training books and seminars. *"Show them!"*

Seems such a device works well in witnessing too. Here's an illustration of someone who used it to good effect.

Jim, a church elder, was asked to oversee the evangelism of new people moving into the community. Sun Lee and his family had just arrived, penniless and alone, as refugees from Vietnam. They needed help immediately.

"First, we've got to get you some food," Jim said, helping the family settle into their small, sparsely furnished apartment. "Then we'll try to find you a good job."

The head of the household nodded and smiled, not knowing what the man was saying. None of the new arrivals spoke a word of English.

Time passed. Sun Lee went to work. The two men tried to communicate, even attempting to learn a few words in the other's language, but progress was slow. Jim longed to tell his friend about Jesus, about how He'd died for the sins of the world, but he just couldn't get the beautiful truths of salvation across without knowing Vietnamese.

One day, after studying the language for many weeks, Jim decided to introduce Sun Lee to his Savior. He tried to explain about God and Jesus, but the more he talked, the more confusing everything seemed to get. Sun Lee would repeat in Vietnamese a little of what Jim said then try to translate the words into English, but somehow the meaning wasn't getting through.

"I can't do this," Jim moaned, a sad smile creasing his face. "It's just not working. How will I ever reach you?"

Sun Lee thought for a moment, then blurted, "Jesus. He like you, Jim? If He like you, I want know Him."

For months, Jim had been trying to communicate the gospel through words. But his actions—his kindness and concern for the little family who'd come to a strange new world—had demonstrated in living color and stereo sound the character of Christ. His life had been a sermon, and Sun Lee had been listening, learning, and understanding far more than Jim imagined.

As we discovered earlier, God had been telling the world about the plan of salvation for centuries. While prophets attempted to pass on the truth as they heard it, Heaven's communications had been derailed by human limitations, clouded by human emotions, and constantly altered by human interpretations.

Then, one day, the telling ceased. There stood a Man, a perfect Man who would *show* in no uncertain terms what God had been trying to say.

Christ's life was a living, breathing sermon, the gospel delivered in pure form without human rendering. Truth shone through His actions and, to this day, provides a standard by which we can judge all other truths, even those contained in the Written Word.

As any good communicator or Christian trying to share his or her faith with others knows: many times, you have to show, not tell.

* * * * *

The You Saga

The moment arrives, and you're not ready.

You've been warned! " 'You are my witnesses,' declares the LORD, 'and my servant whom I have chosen' " (Isaiah 43:10).

You've even been given the topic to discuss. " 'You are my witnesses,' declares the LORD, 'that I am God' " (verse 12).

Now, here it is. Your friend has asked *the* question and is waiting for an answer: "Why do you believe in God?"

Suddenly, all the sermons, classroom lectures, articles, and conversations about witnessing you've endured vanish from your memory like a midmorning San Francisco fog. You're left with the uncomfortable realization that you don't know why you believe in God.

You also realize that the simple statement "Because I just do" or "Because my mommy and daddy told me to" probably won't fly in this situation. It's adult time, and your companion expects a rational, grown-up answer.

Admitting to a belief in God requires a genuine leap of faith. There's no logical proof that He exists. You can't exactly take your friend by the hand and introduce him or her to the Creator of the universe. "Sam, God. God, Sam." Not going to happen.

Also, convincing someone to tag along with you to church may or may not help matters either. At best, church is where God is talked about, sung about, and prayed to—all worthy efforts. But it may not provide the revelation needed in this situation. Same with dropping a God-themed book or website address into outstretched hands. They simply reveal why someone *else* believes in God. The question was: "Why do *you* believe?"

I'm going to let you in on a little secret—one that most people fail to fully appreciate. This often-overlooked detail can sweep away any uncertainty you may have about witnessing for your faith and can become a powerful tool when responding to that all-important question. It has to do with what's going on inside your mind.

As I mentioned, I've lived in many countries of this world, and all were filled with people whom I got to know on one level or another. Shopkeepers, taxi drivers, students, neighbors, friends: each proved one rather uncontroversial fact. No matter where I lived, no matter what social or economic reality surrounded me, every one of those people was just like me. They laughed at the same silliness I laughed at, cried right on cue with me when something tragic happened, raised their hands in frustration in sync with mine when facing confusing or irrational situations, and—most telling of all—endlessly wondered at the randomness of life and our place in it just as I do.

If you scratch below skin color or political leanings, brush aside the heritage that forms cultures, and ignore those things that serve as the meaningless trappings of life, what do you have? You have *you*!

So, if we're to become witnesses, if we're to be mouthpieces for the Almighty tasked with revealing the existence and purpose of God, the most effective training ground for accomplishing that vital undertaking is right in our own minds. As we rummage around our own imperfect and seemingly worthless lives, we discover a vibrant connection with every other human being on this planet. Our witness is, in reality, to ourselves!

So, why do you believe in God? Well, why do you listen to Christian music from time to time? Why do you have this nagging urge to be of service to humanity? Why is it that when you see someone in need—someone struggling with an issue of life, someone in emotional pain—you want to step in and do something? The answer is simple. You're in training. Witnessing school is in session right in your brain. The sooner we all realize this, the better.

Witnessing is sharing what God has done for you, not what you think He can do for someone else. You can't possibly know how God will deal with another person's problem. You don't know the methods He'll use to reach inside that individual's heart and create something new—something beautiful. You just know what He's done for you.

When you share your story, you're bringing hope to others. They quickly realize that there's a power in this universe that can reboot lives and bring healing. Your training has made you a visual aid for God, allowing others to catch a glimpse of what He can do for them.

So, the next time someone asks, "Why do you believe in God?" you can be ready with your answer. You might begin with these words: "Let me tell you a story." Then offer a condensed version of the You Saga. Don't hold back. End with, "And He changed me when I couldn't change myself." Then, add this simple invitation: "I'm sure God has an awesome plan for you too."

And relax! This witnessing? You've already trained for it.

* * * * *

Fitness for Service

A schoolboy was trying out for a play. His mother, seeing how set he was on getting a part, feared he might not be chosen and that the decision would crush him emotionally.

She arrived at the school on the day the parts were awarded. The boy rushed up to her, eyes shining with pride and excitement. "Mommy, Mommy," he shouted breathlessly. "Guess what?"

"What?" the mother asked as she hugged her son, hoping against hope that her precious offspring wasn't given a part he didn't like.

The young child smiled broadly. "I'm in the play! I've been chosen to clap and cheer!"

God bestows upon members of His church—especially those who long to be a witness for their faith—an endless stream of spiritual gifts. According to the Bible, these gifts may include abilities and talents, mental strengths, spiritual insights, and even the rare capability of peering into the future. The Bible suggests in 1 Corinthians 12:31 that we desire, or covet, the "greater gifts," which means we should strive to develop and perfect them in our lives.

As wonderful and desirable as spiritual gifts may be, there might be more to them than meets the eye.

On a snowy morning at five o'clock, a candidate for missionary service rang the bell at the home of the church leader who assigned and coordinated overseas appointments. The visitor was ushered into the parlor, where he sat for three hours beyond the time that his interview had been scheduled. At long last, the administrator appeared and began his questioning.

"Can you spell?" the officer of the church asked.

Somewhat mystified, the candidate nodded. "Yes, sir."

"Fine. Spell *baker*."

"B-A-K-E-R."

The examiner made a mark in his notebook. "Do you know anything about numbers?"

"Yes, a bit."

"Good. Please add two plus two."

"Four."

"Great." The questioner stood to his feet. "I believe you've passed. I'll inform the church board tomorrow. You'll be hearing from us soon."

At the board meeting, the administrator gave his report of the interview. He said, "The candidate has all the qualifications of a fine missionary. First, I tested him on self-denial, making him arrive at my home at five o'clock in the morning. Second, I tested him on promptness. He rang the bell exactly on the hour. Third, I examined him for patience by making him wait for three hours to see me. Fourth, I tested him on his temper. He showed no anger or aggravation. Fifth, I tried his humility by asking him questions any seven-year-old could answer, but he showed no resentment. Yes, I believe the candidate meets the requirements perfectly."

It's my opinion that when God showers spiritual gifts on His people, He's accomplishing far more than providing a way to spread the good news of salvation throughout the world. He's also creating an avenue by which He can obtain a clear indication of our fitness for service and our willingness to use whatever gift we have to glorify His name. "So Christ himself gave the apostles, the prophets, the evangelists, the pastors and teachers, to equip his people for works of service, so that the body of Christ may be built up" (Ephesians 4:11, 12).

He wants more than our hands and feet out there in the wild. He wants our hearts and minds as well. All are important to our witness to the world.

* * * * *

The Guide—Part 1

"You are my witnesses," declares the Lord.

—Isaiah 43:10

One cold morning during a visit to the city of Jerusalem, I got up before my parents and sister to discover that during the night, a blanket of snow had fallen, covering the ground with soft, white folds. My teenage heart yearned for adventure, so I slipped into my warmest clothes, left the guest room we were staying in, and hurried to the Damascus Gate. The narrow streets of the old city waited peacefully in the half-light of dawn.

After exploring the mountaintop that served as the foundation of Solomon's temple millennia ago, I found myself roaming across the Kidron Valley and climbing the Mount of Olives. With deep reverence, I passed through the front gate of the Garden of Gethsemane and found a place to rest beneath gnarled and twisted olive branches. My imagination was working overtime, trying to fill in the visual gaps separating me from the time of Christ when He walked the same paths and sat beneath the same branches.

Suddenly I heard footsteps. A man, probably in his early twenties, shuffled up beside me, a friendly smile lighting his weather-tanned face. "Hello," I said in my best Arabic.

He nodded, then motioned for me to follow.

"Where are we going?" I asked. He just smiled and began walking, his worn boots crunching in the newly fallen snow.

We climbed the hill in silence. Each time I tried to begin a conversation, he'd just nod, pulling his threadbare coat closer about him as the cold wind whispered through the Kidron. *My Arabic must be pretty bad*, I thought to myself. I tried English. No luck. He simply smiled and continued leading me along the winding road.

Before long, we came to a small church perched on the hillside. He pointed up at it and tilted his head questioningly.

Inside the little structure waited display cases filled with handwritten portions of Scripture. I recognized names on the displays' information cards like "Isaiah", "Jeremiah", "Psalms", and others. But it was the stranger's expression that captivated my attention. He'd run his hand along the smooth glass separating him from the sheets of faded parchment as if he were touching something of great value. Such reverence. Such deep affection for those ancient writings.

Apparently, this wasn't the only stop he wanted us to make. He motioned for me to follow, and we left the little building and began our climb once again. Where were we going? What was I supposed to see?

Soon we were standing at the very top of the mountain opposite the city, gazing down at the walls encircling Jerusalem. "It's beautiful," I gasped. "Look how the snow makes everything so clean and—"

The words caught in my throat. The man beside me was quietly crying.

* * * * *

The Guide—Part 2

Show me your ways, Lord,
teach me your paths.
Guide me in your truth and teach me.

—Psalm 25:4, 5

Tears trickled down the stranger's cheeks as he stood at my side, gazing at the ancient city of Jerusalem. His eyes seemed so filled with sorrow. I figured that something terrible must have happened to him within those cold stone walls. "Why?" I asked softly. "Why are you crying?"

The stranger looked over at me, and I saw that the anguish had passed, replaced by a tired and kindly smile. Once again, he motioned for me to follow.

He led me to a small café in an old building by the edge of the road. The warmth inside felt good to my face and hands, and the dim recesses of the room provided a welcome relief from the early morning brightness.

"I see you've met my brother," an older gentleman with a thick Arabic accent called as I sat down near the window. "He's the best guide in Jerusalem. Been taking tourists up and down the Mount of Olives for years."

"But he doesn't ever say anything," I sighed. "Does he know English?"

The older man walked to my table and took a seat across from me as my mysterious self-appointed guide busied himself preparing cups of hot chocolate at the counter. "You're not the first visitor to find that a bit puzzling," he said. "You see, my little brother doesn't talk because he can't. He's never said a single word. Doctors call it a birth defect. They say he'll never be able to speak. Not ever."

The younger sibling placed a steaming cup before me with a satisfied grin and then hurried to the door. With a wave, he was gone.

"Heading out to look for someone else to lead up the mountain," his brother announced with pride lifting his words. "Works from sunup to sundown."

"But," I protested, reaching into my pocket, "I didn't pay him yet."

"Wouldn't do any good to try," the man said, raising his hand. "He never asks for money. You see, my brother's a Christian and believes God wants him to spend his life showing visitors the beauties of the mountain. It's like his witness. His . . . silent witness."

Today, whenever I think of Jerusalem, I picture two men climbing the Mount of Olives. One is Jesus, the Son of God, walking the narrow paths and knowing full well He'll be betrayed and crucified by the very people He came to save.

The other is a kind, weatherworn stranger with a threadbare coat and friendly smile who demonstrates daily that the sacrifice of the first still changes lives today and brightens the way for anyone willing to experience the silent witness of redeeming love.

PART 4

The HEART of SERVICE

Amazing teens give back to their communities.

Sharing God

So far in this book, we've learned that, out there in the wild,

1. you and I are at the center of a cosmic conflict between good and evil,
2. God isn't who many say He is based on Satan and his endless stream of lies, and
3. we've been given the privilege and honor to share the real truth about God—as revealed by the life of Jesus—through our witness.

Now, I'd like to turn our attention to some prime examples of young people who are demonstrating (showing, not just telling) the love of Christ to their communities. That may or may not have been their initial motivation. In fact, some of these mission-minded individuals may not even be Christian. But I suggest that God's love is God's love no matter who is expressing it or why.

Say you're injured, and an ambulance rushes you to the emergency room. Do you ask to see the church attendance record or baptismal certificate of those offering lifesaving care to you? Hardly! Your doctor can be an atheist or worship caterpillars if that's what suits him or her. But you'll receive the very same professional and effective attention you need, and you're very thankful for the doctor's service. You praise God that he or she was there for you.

It's the same with the stories you're about to read, which took place during the past decade or so. No matter what drives these young people—be it Christian ideals or humanitarian morals—the result is the same. God's love is demonstrated.

To paraphrase Shakespeare, "God's love, by any other name, would still bless people."

When we share love, we're sharing a glimpse of God.

* * * * *

What's in Your Hand?

I'm reminded of a Bible story you may have heard many times. Moses, hiding out in the desert after fleeing Egypt (he was running from the law because he'd stopped a slave from being beaten by an overseer by killing the overseer), comes face-to-face with God. Seems the Almighty wanted Moses to return to the capital and demand that His people be allowed to leave that enslaving nation for a promised land far to the north.

Moses asked, "What if they do not believe me or listen to me and say, 'The Lord did not appear to you'?" (Exodus 4:1).

The Lord was ready with an impressive visual aid:

> Then the Lord said to him, "What is that in your hand?"
>
> "A staff," he replied.
>
> The Lord said, "Throw it to the ground."
>
> Moses threw it on the ground and it became a snake, and he ran from it. Then the Lord said to him, "Reach out your hand and take it by the tail." So Moses reached out and took hold of the snake and it turned back into a staff in his hand. "This," said the Lord, "is so that they may believe that the Lord, the God of their fathers—the God of Abraham, the God of Isaac and the God of Jacob—has appeared to you" (verses 2–5).

OK. That's convincing!

There's a lesson here for those who question how we can be of service to our fellow travelers. God asks, "What's in your hand?" In other words, "What are your skills, your talents, your passions? What do you know? What can you do?" Our answer can serve as the foundation for an entire life of witnessing and service.

When I was a teen, my hands held a camera, played the piano, or wrote stories. I had a passion for airplanes and sharing God's love with people. I built a career around those things that continues to this day. The same can happen to you. What's in your hand?

Let's see how that concept has played out in the lives of some very passionate teens—and a few younger folks as well! Who knows? Their stories may inspire you to make a difference—in your own special way—out there in the wild!

* * * * *

Hairy Hugs

What do you do when you want to help sick people but don't have any money? Six brothers found the answer waiting on the top of their heads.

When a family friend died of cancer, the sons of Phoebe Kannisto wanted to do something to show their love and support for others who may be fighting this sometimes deadly disease. So, they—along with their mom—did something unusual. They stopped getting their hair cut. They allowed their hair to get longer and longer for two years.

Yes, some schoolmates made fun of them . . . until the reason for their lengthy locks became known.

At long last, when they decided that their hair was just the right length, they showed up for a haircut with one request. "Cut our hair back to normal length," they stated, "but don't throw it away." Instead, every inch of their long hair was carefully collected, packaged, and sent to an organization called Children With Hair Loss.

After all the snipping and clipping was done, the Kannisto family's collection of "hairy hugs" measured seventeen feet! Off to Children With Hair Loss their gift went, ready to be made into beautiful hairpieces given without cost to financially disadvantaged children under age twenty-one. These boys and girls may be suffering from long-term hair loss due to a number of medical conditions, including cancer.

Sometimes the treatment for certain diseases and the diseases themselves can make a person's hair fall out. Children With Hair Loss offers hairpieces expertly created from donated hair to cover the heads of those who would otherwise be totally bald. These hairpieces help restore self-esteem and confidence so these young people can face the world and their friends with a smile.

What's next for the Kannisto brothers and their mom? They say they're planning to grow out their hair for another donation. They're hoping that their baby sister will join the campaign, too—just as soon as she's old enough to produce hairy hugs of her own.

* * * * *

Sharing Your Voice

Autumn Uhrig, a student at a Christian academy in Maryland, leaned just a little closer to the screen as a YouTube video played. It was showing her that the ability to speak out loud was a gift not everyone shared. Because of accidents, disease, or heredity, there were those for whom the simple act of talking to a friend, singing a song, debating a point, or even asking someone to pass the salt wasn't possible.

Many of these people had to depend on text-to-speech devices to communicate. One problem. These electronic wonders sounded the same whether the user was eight or eighty, male or female.

Wouldn't it be great if these people could have their very own voice? Autumn thought. *They could at last speak to the world in a unique way, just like everyone else.*

After a little online research, the girl discovered that her dream for those who can't speak for themselves could come true with a little help from . . . her! There was a company called VocaliD that was, as their website proclaimed, "the human voicebank of the world."

Autumn's research showed her that this amazing organization already had fourteen thousand speakers representing 110 countries on file. They'd recorded more than six million sentences, which were stored in an ever-expanding voice bank. *I could do that,* Autumn thought to herself, rubbing her chin with the back of her fingers. *I could become someone's voice!*

She learned that the process of sharing speech wasn't exactly quick or painless. It would demand many hours of her time. For a busy academy student, free time was not exactly something she had in abundance. But she remembered the robotic sounds of the devices people who could not speak for themselves were forced to use, and she determined to find the time and do the work no matter what.

VocaliD takes recordings of human voices, blends them using advanced technology with sounds a nonspeaking person can make, and then creates a unique humanized voice ready to become that person's vocal identity.

The process began with Autumn recording just a few sentences so that potential users could hear what she sounded like. In other words, if there was a speech-impaired young female somewhere in the world, she could listen to Autumn's recording and say to herself, *Hey! That girl sounds like me!*

After Autumn submitted her sample statements, she received an email from a girl named Tesa. The young lady felt that Autumn's voice best represented what she wanted to—or used to—sound like.

Now the hard work began. "I would come home from school every day, do my homework, and then go to a quiet room to record as many sentences as I could before bed," Autumn remembers. How many sentences did it take to complete the project? Three thousand, four hundred and eighty-eight to be exact! That's a lot of talking. "At the end of each session, my throat would hurt a little bit, but it was worth it."

Autumn's experience was a little more intense than some because VocaliD hoped to give Tesa the gift of unique speech by Christmas of that year. They—and Autumn—made it happen. On that special day, Tesa was able to say "Merry Christmas" and "I love you" to her family—and to Baby Jesus—in her own, special way using her own unique voice.

But Autumn's words aren't finished yet. Tesa got her very own voice, but other girls will also benefit. Her recordings can serve as the foundation for anyone who believes her sound is compatible with theirs. "Currently, there are three young women considering my voice as a match," reports a very happy Autumn. "Though it took a long time to do—it was actually pretty exhausting at times—it was well worth it," the voice donor insists. "Those women will get their own voice, and I had a part in giving it to them."

Perhaps God had Autumn and Tesa in mind when He said,

> They have no speech, they use no words;
> no sound is heard from them.
> Yet their voice goes out into all the earth,
> their words to the ends of the world (Psalm 19:3, 4).

* * * * *

Cold Caring

Minnesota winter nights can get downright nippy.* Just ask seventeen-year-old Plymouth native Peter Larson. For the past twelve years, this young man has spent forty consecutive nights each winter—during November and December—camping out in his backyard, all by himself, in a box. A *cardboard* box.

"You don't know what cold is until the middle of a December night in Minnesota," Peter says. "Some nights, I'm afraid that my hair will freeze to my head."

Why would someone with a perfectly good and comfortably heated bedroom just a few paces away do such a thing? "I do this every year to build awareness that, even in my town, there are people who are homeless," he states. "Most of us see them every day but never really realize their circumstances."

What sparked this deep interest in those who call the streets home? When Peter was six, he met Bob Fisher, a veteran winter camper and the founder of the Sleep Out Campaign. Bob was teaching Peter's Cub Scout troop about winter camping and revealed to them the hidden world of the homeless. "I told the kids what it feels like to sleep out in the freezing cold," Fisher states. "I explained how, when [the Scouts] leave their tents the next day, they can go home to their nice warm beds and play [their computer games] and have a warm shower and a good meal. But what would it be like if you're a homeless child and had to sleep out like this every day?"

Fisher explained that for every $500 raised, his organization could provide one family with housing assistance. That was all Peter needed to hear. He immediately searched the congregation of his home church for sponsors willing to pay him to sleep out in the cold.

* Information about Peter's story can be found here: Marta W. Aldrich, "Teen Has Heart for the Homeless," *American Profile*, December 17, 2009, https://americanprofile.com/articles/teen-sleeps-outdoors-to-raise-homelessness-awareness/.

During the past twelve years, Peter has raised more than $500,000! Simple math reveals that this future computer science major has put a warm roof over the heads of at least one thousand families. "One person can really make a huge difference," Peter says, "even if they start small."

And that's a cold, hard fact.

* * * * *

Handyman

For the first time in his life, nine-year-old Matthew Shields can high-five his friends, thanks to a smart, caring teenager and a 3D printer.

Matthew was born without fingers on his right hand. His mother, Jennifer, noticed that her son's defect made him self-conscious at school. Classmates would point, stare, or even sometimes giggle at his deformity. This broke her heart and made her son feel uncomfortably different.

A "fake hand" called a prosthetic would help, but it was far too expensive. She uncovered detailed plans for just such a device on the internet but didn't know how to build it.

That's when Mason Wilde, a junior at nearby Louisburg High School in Kansas, stepped in. This straight-A student with dreams of becoming an engineer downloaded the files and headed straight to his local library. He knew that he'd find just what he needed waiting among the many books—a 3D printer!

It took eight hours for the printer to melt plastic filament and create the twenty pieces necessary to create the hand. Mason assembled everything using nylon cord and stainless-steel screws. Then he mounted the device on a glove-like cuff carefully molded to fit Matthew's fingerless hand. Total cost for materials? Sixty dollars.

Matthew soon learned to use backward and forward movements of his wrist to open and close his new fingers. "It's awesome," he says. "I could climb a gigantic mountain. Maybe I could clean my room faster."

Now the kids at school don't tease him. Instead, they point at his new hand and say, "Hey, that's cool!"

Engineer-in-training Mason isn't finished with his Robohand project. He has established a nonprofit organization to help raise funds to buy his very own 3D printer so he can make prosthetics for other people who need them. "It's an amazing feeling to be able to give someone a hand," he tells people.

Matthew agrees and will happily share a high-five to prove it.

* * * * *

Ho Ho Reece

By the time he was nine years old, Reece Davis had spent one hundred days in the hospital. Even though his family and friends visited him often, he knew how lonely nights could be and how scary the quiet halls of the cancer ward became after everyone had gone home.

Holidays were the worst. While everyone else was out having fun, he had to remain securely in bed, battling a tumor with a name he could barely pronounce. He wondered how many of his old buddies knew what *neuroblastoma* meant.

Reece survived his ordeal, went home, and got on with his life. But those hospital memories remained. That's why, last Christmas, that young boy walked right back into Children's Mercy Hospital in Kansas City, Missouri. This time, he wasn't carrying a tumor inside him. This time, he was carrying an armload of brightly wrapped presents. Eighty-four toys, to be exact.

"I have heard that some kids don't have parents here and so they can't play with stuff," he told reporters.

Where did he get all those toys? He held a toy drive and invited his friends to help. Other people donated money, and Reece went on a shopping spree with his dad. "I'm very proud of him," his father said. "This is the start of a tradition."

Reece Davis is following in the footsteps of many, many people—old and young alike—who've been healed of a terrible disease. When they discovered that their pain and fear had subsided, they suddenly found themselves with a great desire to share love and hope with others. Sometimes a lifetime of witnessing can come from a walk in the shadows of fear and uncertainty.

* * * * *

Katie's Krops

It began with a cabbage. A very, very, very *big* cabbage.*

Years ago, Katie Stagliano brought home a cabbage seedling for a third-grade science project. After a lot of watering and weeding, that little seedling

* Information about Katie's story can be found here: Sandy Summers, "S.C. Girl Finds Goodness in Gardening," *American Profile*, August 2, 2011, https://americanprofile.com/articles/south-carolina-girl-gardens-to-help-hungry/.

grew into a forty-pound veggie monster.

Knowing that her big cabbage was a whole lot more than her little family could eat, she lugged it to a local soup kitchen, where she noticed a long line of people waiting for what might be their only meal of the day.

Katie was invited to chop, cook, and serve her cabbage over beds of rice. On that day, 275 hungry diners were glad she showed up.

This gave her an idea. If that simple, homegrown vegetable could feed so many people, how many could a whole garden of vegetables feed? She determined to find out. That's how Katie's Krops was born.

Hearing about her passion for helping the hungry, her school offered a small patch of land for her project. So did local farmer Bob Baker. "You meet somebody at her age who's interested in anything, it's wonderful," Bob reported. "After the cabbage, the seed was planted and she saw a need."

Before long, the people of Summerville, South Carolina, noticed Katie—and some hardworking friends—lugging not just cabbages to the soup kitchen but also beans, carrots, corn, eggplant, herbs, lettuce, melons, okra, rutabagas, squash, and strawberries. The number of hungry people Katie helped feed quickly moved from the hundreds to the thousands.

"God let her know how to grow food," her mother says.

Over the years, Katie bought supplies with the money she raised. She raised so much money that she's been able to provide grants to other young gardeners from Arkansas to Wisconsin. "I wanted them to be really motivated, in their hearts," she says.

Her whole family has been changed by her actions. "I don't think any of us imagined what this would be now, with that one cabbage, how attached she was to it," her mother reports.

Katie has found something else to be attached to. Hungry neighbors.

* * * * *

Llama Mama

Sophia Oster dreams of being a veterinarian. But until that day arrives, she's found an interesting way to enjoy animals and learn a few things along the way.

"I want to bless the town with a petting zoo," she told her mother a few years back. Taking stock of the available critters on the family farm in Fredericktown, Ohio, the girl quickly launched Sophia's Petting Zoo and took her show on the road.

Rolling up their sleeves in support of the girl's mission, the family loaded a collection of chickens, goats, rabbits, and even a llama named Jasmine into the family minivan and began showing up at community events.

The petting zoo was an instant hit. "All the kids really liked it," Sophia reports. "They especially liked the rabbits, since they could hold them."

These days, the Oster's twenty-three-acre farm is home to fifteen chickens, two goats, two horses, six llamas, eight rabbits, and twenty-four sheep. Sophia loves to take part of their menagerie to church socials, birthday parties, nursing homes, or anywhere else people invite her to come. She charges sixty to seventy dollars per event and keeps careful records of her expenses. "I like seeing the kids when they come, watching them hold the animals," she says. "They really don't have the chance to be around animals."

Mom and Dad are more than happy to support their daughter's efforts. "It's just a good experience for her," Sophia's homeschooling mom insists. "It's learning community service, it counts as school, and it's good business training."

With matching funds from her father, Sophia has been able to construct an eight-by-eight-foot holding pen complete with a pink wooden sign identifying "Sophia's Petting Zoo" in yellow letters. The minivan has been relieved of its messy duty by a nice, sturdy trailer.

Sophia's zoo-on-wheels brings a touch of farm life to hundreds of children each year while providing an opportunity for one future veterinarian to generate love and respect for God's beautiful and gentle creatures.

* * * * *

Hugs for Heroes

Back in 2004, Bailey Reese had an idea.*

Hurricane Ivan had just devastated parts of her home state of Florida. When it was safe to do so, she and her mother hurried to a checkpoint where military service personnel were handing out much-needed water and ice. There, she overheard many people in line complaining to the soldiers about having to wait, the inconvenience of it all, and the heat. *They should be thanking those soldiers instead of complaining*, she thought.

This got her thinking. There was a war raging in Iraq at that time, and Bailey couldn't help but believe that American soldiers might appreciate a

* Information about Bailey's story can be found here: Sandy Summers, "Hugs for Heroes," *American Profile*, November 9, 2008, https://americanprofile.com/articles/bailey-reese-hugs-for-heroes/.

little thank-you from people in their homeland so far away. So, she got busy and started collecting sweet treats of gratitude to send—little boxes filled with candies. She ended up shipping about fifty packages overseas.

Her friends quickly caught the spirit of the project and joined in. Soon, more and more boxes of what Bailey called Hero Hugs were on their way to tired, war-weary soldiers. She even decided that the troops needed a mascot, so she created a little stuffed bear and dressed him in Army fatigues. Off to Iraq went Hero for his "tour of duty." The real troops loved Hero and took pictures of him "working" at different posts.

By the time she was twelve years old, her attempts to balance school, cheerleading, and Hero Hugs became overwhelming. So, she quit cheerleading. She also began to receive awards for her efforts, even meeting the president of the United States. But all the attention didn't impress her much. "Taking care of our soldiers and saying thanks is something everyone should be doing," she insisted. "It isn't something special. The soldiers are the ones who deserve recognition for all they sacrifice and give—not me."

Spoken like a true hero.

* * * * *

Music and Smiles

When Alexis Kusy was fourteen years old, her beloved grandmother was diagnosed with Alzheimer's disease.* The condition robs a person of one of his or her most cherished treasures—memories.

Alexis would visit Grandma in the nursing home, but the woman hardly knew her. Gone were the baking days before Christmas. Gone was the warmth of shared family traditions.

That's when the Franklin Lakes, New Jersey, teenager discovered something very interesting. One day, while visiting her grandma, she sat down at the nursing home's piano and started aimlessly playing a tune to pass the time. Suddenly, her usually silent grandmother started laughing, dancing, and singing right along with the Broadway tunes and Christmas carols Alexis was playing. The transformation was amazing!

Not only that, but others in the home also began to join in. The somber room was changed from a quiet, sad place to a joy-filled musical review.

---

* Information about Alexis's story can be found here: Laurel Holliday, "Teen Brings JOY to Nursing Homes," *American Profile,* June 1, 2003, https://americanprofile.com/articles/nursing-home-music-program-joy/.

Alexis had learned firsthand what psychologists have known for some time. Music can reach people who have trouble connecting with other aspects of the world. Even stroke patients (those who've had a blood clot shut off oxygen to a part of their brain) who've been unable to speak can often *sing* the lyrics to familiar songs.

Thrilled that her music had reopened the doors of communication with her grandmother and other patients, Alexis recruited eager schoolmates to join her for a Christmas musical performance at the nursing home. They called themselves JOY, which stands for Joining Old and Young.

JOY went on to perform at many other nursing facilities and soon had more than a thousand residents as grateful fans. Any donations that JOY received were quickly forwarded to the charity Operation Smile, a program dedicated to providing surgery for facial deformities on children and young adults who otherwise couldn't afford it.

"Playing at nursing homes and fundraising for Operation Smile are all part of the same thing," Alexis says. "They're part of the circle of life, in which young contribute to old, and old contribute to young."

Music and smiles: a healing and very happy combination, thanks to Alexis and friends.

* * * * *

My Own Book

Teenage brothers Kyle and Brady Baldwin love to read. Yes, they like to curl up on the sofa with a good book, but they also like reading *out loud* to young children. It's been that way for years.

This Fairfield, California, duo founded their nonprofit organization to do one very important thing: spread the joy of reading by giving free books to kids who cannot afford to buy them. "When I was told some kids grow up never owning a book, I was shocked," Kyle said.

So, along with his brother, he set up My Own Book to fix that problem. They went around their community, contacting local businesses and libraries, book publishers, bookstores, and other supportive individuals, asking them to provide either books or money. The response was satisfying. They even created a website (myownbook.net) to let people know what's happening with their project. There, visitors are urged to get in on the action either by starting a read-out-loud program in their area or donating new books to the cause.

The boys' mother, Sally, is proud of her sons, saying that she and her husband "support them and offer suggestions, but they do all the work themselves."

"We'd rather read than play video games," Kyle insists.

So committed are they to their program that, if funds run low, they dig into their own pockets to keep things moving. They sell homemade wreaths and eggs from their own chickens.

Over the years, the program has set up chapters in various other states. "My Own Book has had ripple effects," says Barbara Mallon, coordinator of the Gifted and Talented Education program in the West Contra Costa School District. "The child who brought home the book (may have) inspired mom and dad to take literacy courses." Barbara also says that children may not know that they love to read because they were never given a chance to find out.

So far, more than fifty thousand books have ended up in the eager hands of underprivileged children.

* * * * *

Can You Hear Me Now?

When Brittany Bergquist, thirteen, and her brother Robbie, twelve, learned about a soldier from their state serving overseas whose phone bill topped $8,000 because of calls to and from home, they got concerned. "We didn't think it was right that our troops had to pay to call home," Brittany said.

So, they sprang into action. First, they emptied their bank accounts. Then they asked friends to chip in. When they went to the bank to deposit their hard-earned $21, the bank provided a $500 contribution to get the ball rolling.

And roll it did! Since that time, the Bergquist siblings have raised nearly $2 million from donations and the sale of recycled cell phones that they collect. The money is used to buy prepaid calling cards that allow faraway soldiers to place calls without being charged. Each card comes with a handwritten note thanking the recipient for his or her service.

"They can make a big difference in a soldier's morale," reports Quentin Carmichael, twenty-nine, the Bergquist siblings' first cousin who helped distribute cards while stationed in Kosovo. Lieutenant Quentin recalls giving a small stack of cards to a recently divorced soldier who was very worried about his daughter. "Later, he said to me," Quentin says, " 'Sir, being able to talk to my daughter regularly has changed my whole life.' "

Brittany and Robbie organized car washes and bake sales and visited corporate sponsors to promote their cause. One large telecom company pitched in $875,000 worth of calling cards and offered 1,800 of their stores as drop-off sites for used cell phones.

Their parents helped as well. Mother Gail set up a workshop where local students could help with the mailings, and father Bob spent much of his free time working for the cause. "I still get goose bumps when I think about what they started," he says.

Thanks to the Bergquist siblings, when a faraway soldier says, "Can you hear me now?" their family can happily answer, "Loud and clear!"

* * * * *

Care Packages for Kids

It began with a community outreach project. David Adamiee helped his fellow church members prepare packages of clothing and other necessities for children who'd been removed from abusive homes. When the project ended, David's desire to make a difference didn't.

"I decided to make five packs," he remembers. "I thought it would be easy and fun!"

Wrong! Many times, when he'd approach the manager of a store to ask for a donation, he or she would take one look at his youthful face and turn him down flat. Did that discourage David? No way! He kept thinking about the abused children who faced uncertain futures. This would motivate him to head immediately to the next store, and the next, and the next.

At long last, he'd gathered almost enough clothing, toothbrushes, and toys to meet his initial goal. But there was a problem.

David's mother remembers walking into her son's room and finding him spreading his precious car collection out on the bed. "The kids' packs don't have enough toys in them," he announced as he started adding some of his own private treasures to the packs.

"That's when I knew [helping kids] was in his heart," his mother says. "He was lost to this cause."

Over the years, David and his passion for trying to bring a little happiness to abused children have grown. He named his cause Kid Packs of America, and it's now a nonprofit organization that continues to help children who struggle with abuse and broken homes. Thousands of unseen smiles have resulted from his hard work and dedication and the generosity of those who support his cause.

David has always said that making time to volunteer for something you believe in is more than rewarding. It does something deep inside your heart. "It just really makes you feel good," he says, "knowing you're helping someone, someone just like you."

* * * * *

Share the Warmth

At first, Amanda Hendryx's fellow classmates questioned her motives.* "They thought I was just being a goodie-goodie, trying to get people to pay attention to me," she remembers. Once they learned more, they liked her idea, and some even donated their own clothes.

What Amanda was trying to do was provide warm garments for homeless people. "I saw a man pushing all his belongings in a grocery cart," she says. "It really hit me."

That experience on the streets of Reno, Nevada, changed her life. She learned that the man wasn't alone; there were thousands of homeless people throughout her state—many of them children. "The typical homeless person in America is a child," she began telling people. "Over 40 percent of homeless children have been homeless more than once. Over half of homeless children have never lived in their own home."

She posted flyers and set up collection boxes around town—including one at her school—promising to dry-clean and deliver the donations to a Reno mission. She called her project Share the Warmth, and before long, people—and even many businesses—responded. Amanda also organized a fundraising skating party at the town's community center. More than one hundred young people showed up.

What was more amazing was that Amanda and her family didn't even live in Reno. They lived 160 miles away. But that image of the homeless man stayed with her after they visited that celebrated mountain town.

To keep the project going, Amanda worked several part-time jobs and, for two summers, labored on a hay ranch, moving irrigation pipes, raking hay, and tending horses, cows, and dogs. "Most people I know were shocked because they thought what I was doing was guys' work," she says. "I got dirty. It was a tough job. But I enjoyed it."

It's safe to say that many homeless people appreciate her dedication when winter winds blow through the streets of Reno, Nevada.

* * * * *

* Information about Amanda's story can be found here: Laurel Holliday, "Teen Launches Mission to Clothe Homeless," *American Profile*, September 15, 2002, https://americanprofile.com/articles/homeless-clothing-teen-movement/.

Shelby's Mission

"Why do I have to stop when everyone else is playing?" Shelby Roberson would ask her mom.* Shelby wondered why she had to "take glucose, drink juice, or check blood sugar [levels]."

The answer was always the same. "Because you have type 1 diabetes."

This disease, which strikes many young people, results from their bodies not making insulin. Insulin is an important hormone that carries glucose—or sugar—from the bloodstream into the cells, where it's converted to energy. Young people need energy—*lots* of energy—to grow and stay healthy. If you don't have insulin, that sugar can't be turned into fuel to run the body properly. Taking glucose or drinking juice provided a little burst of energy to keep Shelby's body going.

As she got a little older, she began to worry not only about herself but also about any child who has type 1 diabetes. So, she decided to do something radical.

Shelby wrote a letter to some government people in Washington, DC. "It is not enough to learn to live with diabetes," she told them. "We have to find a cure. My mom and dad take great care of me, and they are teaching me to do the same, but great care doesn't guarantee that I won't have eye, kidney, or nerve damage in twenty years."

Shelby had learned that type 1 diabetes can affect the health of many parts of the body. "Maybe I won't be able to have children," she concluded. "A cure is the only guarantee that I pray for."

This letter was written when she was six years old.

The government people in Washington read her letters (she wrote many) and got busy. They organized the first Juvenile Diabetes Research Foundation's Children's Congress, where kids and their parents could meet with government officials and voice their concerns.

Research breakthroughs have offered new hope, but the battle to find a cure continues. You can be sure that Shelby Roberson will always be on the front lines, leading the charge.

* * * * *

---

* Information about Shelby's story can be found here: Marie Hoeffner, "Shelby's Mission to Cure Diabetes," *American Profile*, February 16, 2003, https://americanprofile.com/articles/shelbys-mission-to-cure-diabetes/.

Design With God in Mind

It all began with a school assignment. "Think of a world problem and come up with an idea of how you would solve it," the teacher had instructed. Some suggested donating teddy bears to hospitals, fighting poverty, and designing low-fuel cars—all perfectly fine goals. But thirteen-year-old Grace of De Moines, Iowa, wanted to find the answer within herself. "What can I do *personally* to help the world?" she mused.

Then it clicked. *People need God,* she reasoned, *and God is revealed in the Bible. So, people need Bibles! But Bibles cost money. How can I earn money to buy Bibles to put in people's hands?*

The answer was literally at her fingertips. Grace loved doing crafts. She knitted beautiful scarves and winter hats—some even designed for babies. She enjoyed taking nature pictures with her camera and had a reputation as an up-and-coming jewelry creator. What if she made her art available to the public and used some of the profit from each sale to buy Bibles for people who wanted them?

So, she set up shop on the internet and gave her store a very appropriate name: Design With God in Mind.

The website includes a color photograph of each item she's making available, a reasonable price, and a detailed description. Then her shoppers find these words: "With every item purchased on my Etsy shop, an average of 2–6 Bibles will be donated to people around the world who want a Bible but do not have access or can't afford one."

Seems that the items for sale weren't the only part of the business designed with God in mind. So was the salesperson. Her father, Rob, says, "I'm thrilled that Grace is helping show God's love through the work of her hands."

See for yourself: http://www.etsy.com/shop/DesignWithGodInMind.

* * * * *

Cause of God

As we come to the end of this section of the book, I want to know whether you were inspired by what you read. I sure was when I wrote about these amazing young people doing their thing for love.

That brings me to an important point. It's about working in the cause of God, as some people call it. What exactly does that mean?

It *doesn't* mean you have to be employed by a church organization. It simply means that you're motivated by the divine principles of respect, reverence, and concern for all of God's creatures. I don't care what you do, what position you hold, or where you labor. If you are making this world a better place, you are firmly within the cause of God.

I'm reminded of a quote from one of my favorite Christian writers, Ellen White. Listen to what she said: "He [Jesus] was doing God's service just as much when laboring at the carpenter's bench as when working miracles for the multitude."* As a matter of fact, that quote is printed at the bottom of a beautiful painting by artist Nathan Greene. The image he chose to illustrate that quote shows his vision of Jesus sawing through a long piece of wood in the carpenter shop owned by His earthly father, Joseph. That painting hangs in my home office, right above my Korg N1 music synthesizer and audio workstation. It's looking over my shoulder as I type these words.

God needs plumbers, electricians, medical professionals, pilots, bankers, stock-brokers, public school teachers, sanitation workers, clerks, and other workers, as well as ministers, evangelists, ministry directors, and church administrators. To put it simply, the cause of God needs you to do whatever you can that uplifts and affirms the rights and dignity of your fellow human beings.

When I was a young boy, my dad taught me that familiar Bible verse, "Whatever your hand finds to do, do it with all your might" (Ecclesiastes 9:10). I've tried to follow that advice, and I invite you to do the same. The cause of God needs us.

---

* Ellen G. White, *The Desire of Ages* (Nampa, ID: Pacific Press®, 2005), 74.

PART 5

LOVE *and* SEX *by the* BOOK

It was all God's idea.

Am I in Love . . . Really?

Christian and Maryling stood side by side looking down at the dark, swirling waters of a Miami, Florida, canal. Night was heavy around them—but not as heavy as the feelings pressing against their hearts.

After a final embrace, they stepped out into space and dropped into the fast-moving currents. Neither knew how to swim.

Earlier that evening, Christian Davila, fourteen, had penned a letter to his parents. "I can't go on living," he wrote. "I'm escaping from the realm of reality into the darkness of the unknown. Because reality is, I can't be with Maryling."

Maryling Flores, thirteen, had jotted down her thoughts as well, leaving a letter addressed to her mom and dad. "You'll never be able to understand the love between me and Christian. You don't let me see him in this world, so we're going to another place. Please don't cry for me, this is what I want. I want to feel happy, because I'm going to a place where I can be with Christian."

The girl's parents had forbidden her to date Christian anymore, thinking they were far too young to be so serious about each other. Maryling hid an even deeper concern in her heart. She thought she was pregnant—a concern she'd shared with a friend. (It was later discovered she wasn't.)

So, on that night in November 1995, these two young people, seeing no other way out of their dilemma, ended their own lives in a watery canal, leaving behind heartbroken parents, tearful friends, and stunned teachers.

But wait. Weren't they in love? Isn't love worth dying for?

God, the One who created this very powerful emotion called love, inspired these words: "If I speak in the tongues of men or of angels, but do not have love, I am only a resounding gong or a clanging cymbal" (1 Corinthians 13:1).

Then follows a description of this heaven-ordained phenomenon that every teenager and adult should know backward and forward. If Christian and his friend Maryling had fully understood the next words, they'd be alive today. Listen to what the Bible says: "Love is patient, love is kind" (verse 4).

It wasn't love that pushed those two teenagers into the canal that night, for love waits; it regroups; it finds a way no matter how long it takes or what obstacles must be overcome.

It wasn't love that created the headlines, got the coroner out of bed, and took away the joy of so many people. Love is kind. It never hurts others.

So, what did Christian and Maryling have? What drove them to end their lives that horrible night?

The answer is complicated and often elusive. But it does exist, partially in

God's Word and partially in the human heart. If you stay with me, we'll dig together to find the hidden treasures of truth we all need to know.

* * * * *

What Did God Have in Mind, Anyway?

It began in Eden, that beautiful garden God created for Earth's first lovers, Adam and Eve. After Adam's emotions had settled down a bit from seeing his newly formed bride for the first time, God invited the happy couple to "be fruitful and increase in number; fill the earth and subdue it" (Genesis 1:28).

What? That's sex! The only way to "be fruitful and increase in number" is to make babies. Was God telling Adam and Eve to have sex? Absolutely!

It seems we've uncovered a rather significant truth already. In Eden, love and sex were interconnected. One didn't exist without the other. This was God's plan for humanity. Many of the qualities Paul penned in 1 Corinthians 13 concerning love would then also apply to sex. Both should be patient, kind, not envious, not boastful, not proud, not rude, not self-seeking. Sex and love, as God designed them, would never delight in evil. They'd always protect and trust (verses 4–7).

But something happened between Eden and today. Something came along that totally messed up the Creator's perfect plan.

"It was Satan!" I can almost hear you say. "*He* caused the problems. *He* made two Miami teenagers who thought they were in love jump into a canal."

Well, not exactly. Satan didn't push those young people into the water. Christian and Maryling, along with millions of teenagers around the world, are victims of a war that began a long time ago in a garden where two lovers decided that God's ideals weren't worth following.

Yes, Satan brought the temptations. He created an atmosphere of confusion. But the hand that plucked the apple and the feet that leaped into the canal were responding to deliberate choices made by minds that had lost sight of God's ideal.

I want better for you, my friend. I want you to have it all: love, sex, romance, a happy, long-lasting marriage, fulfilling relationships, pride in who you are—yes, every one of them! And you can *if* that's what you *choose* for yourself.

Read on carefully, prayerfully. Ask God to fill your mind with proper images of love and sex. Don't settle for Satan's substitute.

* * * * *

The Sexual Being

Sexuality is what defines *male* and *female*. Again, God set the standard. "But for Adam no suitable helper was found. So the LORD God caused the man to fall into a deep sleep; and while he was sleeping, he took one of the man's ribs and then closed up the place with flesh. Then the LORD God made a woman from the rib he had taken out of the man, and he brought her to the man" (Genesis 2:20–22).

Next follows two astounding statements. Listen:

> That is why a man leaves his father and mother and is united to his wife, and they become one flesh.
>
> Adam and his wife were both naked, and they felt no shame (verses 24, 25).

It seems that sexuality

- was created to fill a need,
- began in human flesh,
- brings about a radical change in a person's life when combined with marriage, and
- is nothing to be ashamed of.

According to God's original plan, men and women were designed as a package deal. Through marriage, human sexuality merges into a condition called "one flesh." This joining together forms what I call "home." And only within this home can sexuality be fully expressed without shame.

What's supposed to happen in this union? "Have kids!" I hear you say. Yes, that's part of it. Child-rearing is the ultimate achievement in God's home plan.

But human sexuality is not just about making love and making babies. It's about *uniqueness*. I enjoy being different from my wife. Through the years, I've watched her strengths make up for my weaknesses, and I've seen my simple abilities complement her needs. That's what God had in mind when He said, "They will become one flesh." My wife and I can accomplish much more together than we ever could apart.

We males and females can laugh at our differences, joke about how we react uniquely to certain situations, or even poke fun at the confusion we sometimes feel in dealing with each other. But we must never, *ever* consider someone better, smarter, more qualified, or in any way superior based on whether they wear panties or boxer shorts. To do so is offensive to the God who made us unique by carefully designing our sexuality.

"There is neither Jew nor Gentile, neither slave nor free, nor is there male and female, for you are all one in Christ Jesus" (Galatians 3:28). Different, but the same. Two people, one flesh.

* * * * *

The Purity of the Difference

Looking at sexuality only in terms of the *physical* differences between men and women is like standing with your nose pressed against a tree and saying, "My, what a lovely forest!"

TV programs and movies shamelessly exploit women's bodies. Books and magazines show men as aggressors; the more violent, the better. Advertisers target teens with suggestions that "if you wear these clothes or buy this particular product, it'll make you more attractive to the opposite sex." So, guys begin judging their worth by how many girls they "conquer," and girls think they don't have value unless they're hounded for dates. We make sex the yardstick with which we measure our worth.

The problem is that meaningful friendships, opportunities to practice gentle manners, and discovering important life lessons get trampled by the rush to be totally cool, to be in, hot, with it—or whatever words are used these days. We're standing with our faces pressed against a tree and thinking we're seeing the forest.

Out there in the wild, don't get stuck in this narrow view of sexuality. Place God in the picture. Consider *all* the reasons why He made men different from women. And then preserve and defend the purity of those differences, whatever they may be.

"The body . . . is not meant for sexual immorality but for the Lord, and the Lord for the body" (1 Corinthians 6:13).

Isn't it nice to know that the God of the universe wants you to enjoy your sexuality as long as you use it to fulfill His wonderful plan for your life?

* * * * *

Changes

We've already established that men are different from women, and for this, I'll be eternally grateful. But I'm told that changing from a girl to a woman can be an exercise in abject terror or curious fascination. Thankfully, once you know why something is happening, its "weirdness" diminishes greatly.

That transformation has its roots in a command God gave Adam and Eve. Remember? He said, "Be fruitful and increase in number" (Genesis 1:28). In other words, make babies. To do that, a woman's body must develop in certain ways. Breasts enlarge to accommodate milk production. A monthly cycle of egg creation and release gets underway. Bones and muscles change shape, preparing to provide for the future nine-month construction of a human being.

Stages are happening in the girl's mind too. God is preparing her for her role as wife and mother by strengthening her sensitivity to the needs of others, increasing her desire to be attractive to the same guy she used to beat up on the playground, and awakening thoughts of home and family.

At least, that's the way it's *supposed* to be. This world, with its demands and distractions, can lead a woman in many directions. You have an abundance of choices for your life. But regardless of what path a woman decides to take, God's orderly sequence remains the same. "I will instruct you and teach you in the way you should go," He says (Psalm 32:8). God understands the strange stages of growing up. He can and will help.

Most preteen boys are curious about all the different shapes they see hiding under women's clothes. Then, they see naked bodies in certain magazines and find out what's where. But something also changes in them as they begin to mature into young men.

God placed into man's mind a sexual fascination with and powerful attraction to the female body. In Heaven's original plan, this process was beautiful, wholesome, and natural. A guy would find himself smitten with a particular female, and they'd fall in love, marry, and begin making babies. Case closed.

Sexual attraction was meant to be shared between two people who had chosen to commit themselves to each other for life.

Then along came Satan, who said, "If I can weaken man's mind through disease, bad habits, and disobedience to God's perfect laws, I'll be able to turn sexual attraction into a game, an addiction, even a sin." And that's exactly what he did. "For everything in the world—the lust of the flesh, the lust of the eyes, and the pride of life—comes not from the Father but from the world" (1 John 2:16). Sin is seductive. It also spoils everything.

God wants you to like sex. He gave you the urge to make love. He designed you to enjoy kissing, hugging, petting, and other physical pleasures. But He also created a proper *place* for all this fun stuff to happen. That place is called marriage.

Guys, when you gaze lustfully at a naked woman spreading herself across the staples of a magazine or on a computer screen, you're rejecting God's plan. You're abandoning His ideal for your life and leaving yourself wide open to Satan and his evil temptations.

If you want to enjoy sexual thoughts, then educate yourself, work at becoming a kind and loving person, commit to someone who loves you, get married, and have at it. Share this special love with your wife often. Enjoy sex in the safety and God-blessed sanctuary of your own home. Leave those seductive images to the immature boys who aren't relying on God to live life His way.

* * * * *

Sex and Love for the Long Haul

First, we need to review several often overlooked facts: (1) it's entirely possible to fall in love more than once, (2) it's entirely possible to love someone dearly and not have sex with him or her, and (3) it's entirely possible to have sex with someone and not be in love.

You see, love is demonstrated in many more ways than jumping into bed with someone. Salamanders have sex. So do roses, sort of. But you never see them picking out curtains together. The presence of sexual activity doesn't necessarily indicate the presence of love. Its absence doesn't prove anything either. Love is different things to different people.

However, there are certain guidelines for making a loving relationship the most rewarding, exciting, satisfying experience on earth.

That's why God designed physical intimacy to be enjoyed after marriage. He wanted sex to be an *expression* of love, not an *indicator* of it. Sex was created to be shared between two people who have publicly promised God and each other that their love is forever.

A relationship built on sex has nothing to fall back on in times of trouble—and trust me, trouble always comes. It might be in the form of sickness, stress, disappointment, anger, even old age. These elements can reach into a relationship and snatch away the ability or even desire for sex. But two people who've promised God and fellow human beings that they're going to face the future together still have their love to lift them along. There remain promises to keep and dreams to fulfill.

In my work as a media producer, I sometimes visit retirement villages and nursing homes, preparing marketing tools to help the facilities attract more residents. Often, I interview the people living there, asking them what they like most about the community and the services they receive.

I've seen husbands caring for disabled wives and wives watching over bedridden husbands. To these precious folks, sex is but a memory. But, when you see them together, holding hands, smiling into each other's eyes, laughing, joking, sharing the day, you realize just how powerful love is. Yes, they've had years to refine and strengthen their relationships, but the seeds of love, planted when they first met, have been growing, blooming, and nurturing in ways that physical intimacies can't.

When two people allow love to build first and then bind their lives together in marriage, the sex that follows is simply icing on the cake. Sex doesn't sit up with you when you're sick. Love does. Sex doesn't bring comfort in times of great sorrow. Love does. And when Christ comes the second time, He won't be concerned about how well you performed in bed with your husband or wife. He'll be interested only in how well you loved them—and others.

* * * * *

Love Is Patient

I once had a young person ask, "Hey, Charles, how can I know that I'm really in love?"

Good question. I'd like to spend the remainder of this section checking out some suggestions directly from God's Word for identifying true love. Every attribute is found in 1 Corinthians 13. We'll be using what it says as our guide from here on out. Oh, and remember, since love and sex are directly linked by God, these qualities apply to both equally.

Here's the first suggestion: Are you willing to wait for love to grow without trying to rush it?

One of the hardest things for us human beings to do is wait. I don't like waiting at all! Get me in a long line at the bank or park me on the freeway during rush hour, and I'd rather be *anywhere* else. Why does God insist that love be patient?

Patience is necessary because it often takes time for truth to surface. I know a man and woman who married each other one week after they met. *One week!*

Now they're discovering all sorts of stuff about each other that they didn't know before, things that will keep their relationship from growing and getting stronger. For the rest of their lives, they'll have to settle for a kind of *standoff* relationship, a marriage where no more adjustments will be made to accommodate the other. That's sad.

If they'd been patient, they would have discovered these problems long before they promised God and other people that they'd spend the rest of their lives together. So, my advice to you? Don't be in a big rush. Take your time. Let love simmer slowly.

Let me ask you a question. Would you rather fly in an airplane that someone patched together quickly overnight or in a craft that was assembled carefully, thoughtfully, by a team of people looking for possible flaws along the way?

This patience must also continue to operate at full tilt *after* the *I dos* are uttered. People change. Successful relationships continually adjust to meet new challenges. Love built with patience has a firm foundation on which to stand and make those needed modifications.

Slow down. Build your love over time. It'll make it stronger.

* * * * *

Love Is Kind

Ever heard a guy yell at his girlfriend? Or perhaps you've listened as a girl belittled her boyfriend right in front of everyone. That's not kindness. Those people aren't allowing love to get a foothold in their relationship.

To be kind means to put the needs of the other person first.

As we learned earlier, when a woman who'd been caught committing adultery was brought to Jesus, He allowed love to guide His words. Remember? While everyone else was yelling at her, cursing her actions, telling the world what a sinner she was, our Savior took a very different approach. He gently reminded the accusers that they were guilty of sins of their own. Embarrassed, the angry mob dispersed.

Looking around, Jesus asked, "Woman, where are they? Has no one condemned you?" (John 8:10).

The woman shook her head. "No one, sir," she said.

Quietly, gently, Jesus responded, "Neither do I condemn you. . . . Go now and leave your life of sin" (verse 11).

Whose words do you think that woman remembered? The shouting mob's or Christ's?

When a boyfriend or girlfriend makes a mistake, what motivates your response? If you allow kindness to choose your words and actions, you're feeling true love in your heart.

* * * * *

Love Doesn't Envy

I'm going to let you in on a little secret. I've never been jealous in my relationship with my wife. Is that because I have such a powerful love for her? Well, I do, but that's not the reason. It's because of the power of her love for me. She never does anything to make me feel insecure, unwanted, or rejected. She refuses to create an atmosphere of envy in our relationship, even if I sometimes act like a complete jerk.

Envy can be death to a budding romance.

Girls, let's say you like a guy. He is athletic, has muscles bulging out everywhere, looks like a prince from some Bavarian castle, and can melt your heart with a smile. (Sorry, I don't have his telephone number.)

This fellow is attracted to you too. He says you're cute. You begin hanging out together. But there's a problem. Every time you see another girl within fifty feet of him, you get all worried. You think, *Is he more interested in her than me? Will he run off with someone else while I'm not looking? Am I pretty enough, smart enough, rich enough, funny enough?*

You may not be aware of it, but you're creating an atmosphere of envy in your relationship. You begin trying too hard to keep his attention. You make sly comments about other girls, putting them down, maybe by saying they're all immature airheads. So, instead of the sweet, kind, fun girl he fell for, you're turning into a cold, nasty person who makes more and more demands.

Of course, guys are capable of creating this type of envy atmosphere as well. But the bottom line is that envy destroys relationships: "Resentment kills a fool, and envy slays the simple" (Job 5:2).

Don't let that "simple" one be you.

* * * * *

Love Doesn't Boast

You see him on almost every television situation comedy one time or another. He wears chest-baring shirts, tight jeans, and expensive accessories. This poor guy can't open his mouth without something sexual sloshing out. He's cool. He's hip. He's boastful.

He's also a royal pain!

Boastful people turn my stomach. You can't trust what they say or depend on their actions. That doesn't stop them from telling you how wonderful they are and what a pathetic moron you happen to be.

Puh-leeze!

As you fall in love, something wonderful happens to your attitude toward the person you've trained your sights on. You begin to protect him or her, and that person begins to protect you.

How? First by word, then by deed.

Suddenly, the *character* of your friend takes on more value. You want to guard that part of that person carefully. True love doesn't allow boastful stories filled with sexual overtones to be shared with your friends after your last encounter. The object of your affection doesn't go around making up tales of conquests and victories concerning you either. As love takes root, the purity and wholesomeness of your relationship grow in importance. This strange but beautiful phenomenon is God's way of letting you know you're on the right track!

From that moment on, even your actions serve to protect the character of the other person. Am I saying that sex isn't a consideration anymore? Hardly. Sexual attraction continues to get stronger and stronger. But it's kept in line, getting all primed and ready for when the promises are made, the marriage vows are spoken, and a new home is started with God as a permanent Partner. Remember, this whole love thing was His idea to begin with. He knows how to make relationships *and* sex work best in the wild.

I do think that love allows for some boasting about your significant other. My wife is beautiful, smart, attractive, a great cook, fun to be with, sympathetic, kind, considerate, and my absolute best friend. There. I feel better.

* * * * *

Love Isn't Proud

Pride goes before destruction,
a haughty spirit before a fall.

—Proverbs 16:18

Pride has probably killed more relationships than anything else on earth. Why? Because the very first thing pride does is snuff out the flickering flame of love.

Love can exist only in a heart that puts the interest and well-being of another person first. Pride turns the spotlight onto self, creating darkness beyond its narrow glow where other people easily feel left out, unimportant, rejected.

Years ago, I sat in the fashionably furnished den of a well-to-do friend. His wife of a dozen years had left him that very afternoon to spend the weekend with another man. He had done the same with other women in the past. Their marriage was over.

"Do you see all this, Charles?" he asked with tears rolling down his cheeks. I looked around at the expensive end tables and lamps, big-screen television, deep-pile rugs, grand piano, and crystal chandelier. Just outside, through broad sliding glass doors, waited a bubbling Jacuzzi and sun-sparkled swimming pool. "It's all worthless to me," he said. "Without my Mary's* love, money and things have no value."

That's what pride does. It sucks the value out of everything else. A pride-filled heart can't love another person because it's focused only on self and what it thinks it needs. All else simply doesn't matter. Pride kept my friends from forgiving each other, rebuilding their failing relationship, and patching up their crumbling home life.

If you're interested in a guy or girl simply because being with them boosts your popularity or makes you more attractive in the eyes of others, beware. There's no way love can exist in such a situation.

But if you're willing to let go of your pride and like a person for the beautiful, kind, gentle individual he or she is, then love's got a fighting chance.

* * * * *

Love Isn't Rude

Now, why on earth would God put this statement in His great love chapter? Of course love isn't rude. Everyone knows that!

Well, not quite everyone. Some guys have the odd idea that bossing a girl around, being macho and crude, and behaving like a clueless caveman is the proper way to show love.

Hey, guys, *grow up*!

Jesus Christ, the greatest demonstration of love this world has ever seen, never spoke a rude or unkind word, never embarrassed anyone, never grossed anybody out, and never aimed His frustration at a person directly. When He did show His unhappiness, like that day in the temple when the money changers were making a mockery of the sacred worship services, He focused His attack on what the men were *doing*, not on their characters. Jesus shouted over the din of commerce as tears stung His eyes, " 'My house will be called a house of prayer,' but you

---

* Not her real name.

are making it a 'den of robbers' " (Matthew 21:13). In essence, Jesus said in no uncertain terms, "What you're *doing* here is wrong. Stop this instant!" He didn't say, "You low-down, selfish, good-for-nothing idiots. You have no place in My Father's house!" Nope. That would be rude. That would be unloving.

There's a lesson here for all would-be lovers. Never attack a person. Instead, focus your attention on what the person did or is doing. "When you didn't show up for our date, I got worried that something bad had happened to you." Isn't that a whole lot better than, "You're just a lazy bum who can't even keep an appointment"?

Or, which of these two statements sounds better to you? "When you look at other girls, I get the idea that you're not interested in me anymore." Or, "You're a thoughtless, mean person who doesn't care one bit for me. Why don't you pay more attention to us?"

Rude words and actions have no place in a loving relationship because they easily wound hearts. Express your feelings? Yes! Stand up for yourself? Absolutely. Just don't attack someone with your anger and frustration. When you do that, it's so easy to be rude.

* * * * *

Love Is Not Self-Seeking

Self-seeking is another way of saying *selfish.*

I once heard a young lady mention that ever since she'd allowed her boyfriend to have sex with her, that's all he wanted to do when they were together—no romantic walks by the ocean, no fun dates at the pizza joint, no visits with friends.

What a sad but accurate illustration of selfishness. This guy was thinking only of himself and the pleasure he took at his girlfriend's expense.

By its very nature, love is others-oriented. Would you expect something less of an emotion created by God? Everything that love does benefits others. The greatest joys lovers experience are those that are shared.

Sometimes in my work, I have to travel without my wife by my side. In those situations, I'm pretty pitiful. I work as fast as I can to get the job done so I can hurry home.

Once, before I even met my wife, I was shooting a documentary on a beautiful Caribbean island. The moon was full and yellow, playing hide-and-seek behind white, fluffy, silver-lined clouds. Palm trees swayed to the rhythm of a small band playing on the beach, where the waves swished softly across the sands. It was absolutely magnificent, but I was absolutely miserable. I had no one to share it with.

Love makes everything more exciting, more satisfying, more enjoyable for *both* participants, not just for one.

While walking along that romantic beach, the verse we looked at earlier popped into my mind: "It is not good for the man to be alone" (Genesis 2:18). I shook my head and thought, *You got that right, God!*

* * * * *

Love Isn't Easily Angered

Do you have a temper? I do, unfortunately. Every so often, it rears its ugly head, and I have to pounce on it with all fours.

Most news reports brim with stories of men who forgot to pounce.

Years ago, a house my wife and I lived in sat very close to our neighbor's abode. Almost every night, we could clearly hear the king of the castle yelling, shouting, screaming at his wife. He called her all sorts of names, told her what a horrible person she was, and warned her to straighten up and fly right or he'd get really angry. Yeah, like he was under control now?

We felt so sorry for that poor woman. She worked hard at the office-supply store we frequented, always kept herself pretty for her husband, and never raised her voice once.

So, which of these people demonstrated love? When we allow anger to drive our responses, even concerning things we have every right to get angry over, we're letting go of love.

"A gentle answer turns away wrath, but a harsh word stirs up anger" (Proverbs 15:1).

How two people respond to each other when things get rough is a pretty good indicator of the strength and validity of their love.

* * * * *

Love Keeps No Record of Wrongs

Oh boy. Here's a tough one.

You and your special man are out enjoying a stroll down a city sidewalk. The two of you pass a clothing store, and you say, "Hey, check out that cool sweater. I think it would look nice on me."

Your man chuckles and says, "Are you crazy? It'd make you look like a beached whale, kind of like that green thing you wear."

Now, just how fast are you going to forget that declaration? A year? Two? Never?

Love, as the Bible describes it, forgives and forgets *right now*. Why? Because hurt feelings only get worse as they're remembered over time.

Perhaps your not-so-subtle companion is right. Perhaps you do look like a beached whale in that green thing—in his opinion. The truth is, some styles look better on certain body shapes, and some styles look awful.

The solution to this particular "keeps no record" situation is (1) your special someone learns to be kind in everything he or she says, and (2) you learn to graciously accept the truth even when it's delivered in the worst possible way.

I've worked out a pretty good system in this matter with my wife. After I put on my clothes and think I look just stunning, I saunter past her nonchalantly. If she glances up and says, "Are you going to wear that?" I smile and quickly go change.

Love has a short memory when it comes to mistakes and errors in judgment. "I, even I, am he who blots out your transgressions, for my own sake, and remembers your sins no more" (Isaiah 43:25). Loving words from God Himself.

A loving relationship remembers much but forgets much, much more.

* * * * *

Love Doesn't Delight in Evil

No one in their right mind believes for a second that rape springs from love. Neither does child molestation, sexual perversion, stalking, sodomy, or any other form of passion that takes its cue from the devil.

Love has no place in such activities. Never has. Never will. But don't try to tell the world that. Many people are under the impression that love is somehow wrapped up in every evil delight.

Relationships that include any form of deviant behavior lack true love. A husband who demands sex instead of nurturing it, a wife who wears very revealing clothes in public to grab attention, pornographic magazines piled under the bed, X-rated websites on a Favorites list, all suggest the very real presence of evil in the home.

Yes, evil can be fun, but only for a moment. These activities may seem OK in the beginning, but soon, very soon, you begin to reap the rewards. Heartache, disease, frustration, guilt, and even death are the payback to those who delight in evil instead of concentrating on finding true, pure love.

As you experience relationships, watch for signs that you or your friends are beginning to find pleasure in what the Bible calls sin. But I don't have to worry about you, do I? Your standards are high. You want to know what *true* love is, and you're not going to settle for anything less.

* * * * *

Love Rejoices With the Truth

The more you get to know a guy or girl, the more secret faults begin to float to the surface in the relationship. In other words, the "true you" or the "true person" starts to shine through.

Love doesn't run and hide every time something pops up that doesn't exactly match your own personal requirements. It rejoices at the opportunities presented.

My wife is very shy. I'm not. When we first started dating, she discovered that being with me took some getting used to. She would have to do some things that shy people hate to do—like being up front before a lot of people, aggressively going after business opportunities, meeting clients, sitting in conferences and planning sessions, calling strangers on the phone, and other scary encounters. Those were all part of who I was, and she slowly began to adjust. Why? Because she loved me.

At the 1995 General Conference Session in Holland, she and I were asked to produce an important program to be presented on the second Sabbath afternoon. During the show, which was being beamed by satellite to hundreds of thousands of homes around the world (this was before internet streaming) as well as being watched by sixty thousand people seated in the big auditorium, I suddenly needed to talk with her. She was backstage getting people organized while I was running things out front. I motioned for her to come to one edge of the big stage so I could give her some instructions. Right there, in front of countless people, my shy, timid, sweet little wife walked out in full view of everyone to get her message and then hurried back to deliver it. Satellite, a huge audience, people everywhere, yet there she was with her gentle smile, looking down at me, putting her shyness aside for the good of the cause.

She'd uncovered the truth about me and made the necessary adjustment. She didn't run and hide. She didn't try to make me shy and timid. No, she changed for me. She challenged her lifelong shyness because she loved me.

As you learn about your special friend, don't be put off by your differences. Accept them and rejoice.

* * * * *

Love Always Protects

"Greater love has no one than this: to lay down one's life for one's friends."
—John 15:13

History is filled with stories of people who've done great and noble deeds for others. I'd like to share a family anecdote that took place before I was born. I have two brothers, Bill and Bob. Bill's the oldest.

When they were quite young, it was determined that Bobby needed to have his tonsils removed. He was terrified. But then Billy stepped in and said, "I'll go with you. I'll have mine taken out, too, so you won't be afraid."

Off they went to the hospital together, trembling hands interlocked. No encouragement from my mom or dad seemed to ease their youngest son's apprehension. But, when the older boy spoke, Bobby seemed to relax. "You'll be OK," Billy kept saying. "I'll be right here with you." His bravery was remarkable and was the only thing that kept Bobby calm.

After the short surgery, the two brothers were wheeled back into the hospital room, groggy from the anesthesia. Bobby looked peaceful and quiet as he slept. Moving to Billy's bedside, my parents looked at his soft, sweet face. Suddenly, they saw a tear slip from the corner of an eye and move silently down his cheek. The bravery had been an act. He'd been as terrified as his younger brother. But he'd been there when Bobby needed him most, silently suffering by his side. Billy had put himself at risk because of love.

What are you willing to sacrifice for love? Pride? Personal fears? The things you consider important? People in love have been making sacrifices for centuries.

* * * * *

Love Always Trusts

One of the strongest pillars supporting true love is trust. Can your boyfriend or girlfriend count on you, come what may? Can he or she trust you?

I once got a Dear John letter. Well, actually, it said, "Dear Charles," but you get the picture. It was during a summer internship program while I was in college. I was traveling around the country attending camps for blind children, making a documentary film, and writing press releases about the camps for local newspapers.

Back at school was a girl I really liked. She'd promised to wait for me; said I was important to her; and, no, she wouldn't run off with someone else.

She ran off with someone else.

When I got the letter, I sat down under a beautiful cottonwood tree to read it. Man, what a shock! I moped around for three days.

I'd trusted her. She'd promised.

Then I met a terrific girl at the very next camp, and life quickly regained its value. Such are the ways of young love. But I'll never forget the feeling of betrayal I felt. When someone breaks your trust, it makes you hurt deeply.

True love—the type required for a successful courtship and marriage—is absolutely trustworthy. Although it may get shaken, pounded, cracked, or even chipped, it still stands firm. Like the wise man's house built on a rock, the love God designed for us to utilize rests securely above the storm of life, holding two people away from the ruin of separation and divorce. Trust is the glue that holds lives together.

You know you're in love when you become as trustworthy as a rock. It's also an accurate way to judge whether someone else's love for you is true. Believe me. I know.

* * * * *

Love Always Hopes

Whenever I want an illustration of what this part of the verse means, I just have to glance over at my wife and remember our first year together.

You know how sometimes trouble comes in groups? That happened to us.

Within one month of getting married, I lost a new job (the company failed) and went deeply into debt moving my furniture around the country. Our car self-destructed; I landed flat on my back, sick in bed; and we ended up living in a borrowed trailer, out of work, out of money, out of luck. But, and I thank God for this, I wasn't out of love.

My wife fixed up our little home with what we had, cooked delicious, health-building meals, read to me while I lay under the covers, and spoke endless words of encouragement and comfort. I had nothing to offer her anymore. Nothing. But she believed everything would turn out OK. And it did. After I got well, I found new work and got busy, and we landed back on our feet, running at full speed just like before.

"And hope does not put us to shame, because God's love has been poured out into our hearts through the Holy Spirit" (Romans 5:5).

My wife never lost hope. Why? She loved me. And she still does!

* * * * *

Love Always Perseveres

Wouldn't it be nice if this were a perfect world, where perfect people fell in love and created perfect homes filled with perfect children? Even the dog would be perfect. The Bible wouldn't need to include 1 Corinthians 13. I wouldn't need to write this book. Everything would be, well, perfect.

In such a world, love would not have to persevere. It would just hum along unchallenged and fully supported by everyone involved. However, in this sinful world, true love simply can't exist without this powerful feature. Period.

My wife and I have a little saying that we utter whenever we do something really, really stupid. OK, I utter it when *I* do something really, really stupid. I'll look at her and say, "Do you *still* love me?"

There's a lot of meaning in that little phrase. In essence, we're asking, "In spite of this dumb mistake, in spite of my sinful human nature, in spite of the fact that I deserve to be flung off a cliff, do you love me enough to love me some more?"

The answer is always yes.

Love does not persevere because it always feels invincible or because it sees a great reward looming nearby. It perseveres because God has empowered it with His spirit of forgiveness and hope.

When you see your relationships beginning to last longer and longer, when you find yourself searching for the good among the bad in a person, when your heart gets battered but somehow comes away even stronger than it was before, you're learning to love. You're learning to persevere!

* * * * *

Love Never Fails

First, let me say that love does not require that a person choose to put himself or herself in unnecessary danger as a matter of course. A battered wife should leave her husband and seek the safety of friends or organizations trained to deal with such a tragedy. Likewise, if a young man finds himself being abused by a girlfriend, he should get out of the relationship as fast as possible. Yes, love can survive even these horrible conditions, but nowhere does it say you have to stand with your nose pressed up against it while it's happening.

For the words *love never fails* to work in a relationship, there are several requirements:

- Both people must be committed to the longevity of the relationship.
- God and His standards must be respected and upheld.
- Forgiveness must be exercised regularly.

You see, there are not two types of love out there—one for singles and one for married people. True love is the same for old folks, newlyweds, high school students, and the thirty-something generation.

Dating, getting to know a lot of guys or girls, discovering your feelings, socializing, and casual boyfriend-girlfriend relationships are one thing. These are people you "like" a lot. But, to move from *like* to *love* requires a commitment to longevity. You can't tell someone, "I'm going to love you for the next few hours or until next weekend, then we'll see what happens." Love isn't something you *try*; it's something you hang promises on, commit to, and take seriously. That's why love lasts and lasts and lasts, even in the face of tough problems and powerful challenges.

True love can't exist without God either (or at least using God's principles as the foundation for the relationship). Why? Here it is again—God created love. Love attempted without regard to God or His rules of engagement is like trying to build a skyscraper without blueprints. It might look nice, but I sure wouldn't want to live or work in it. That's why the Bible can make rash statements such as "Love never fails" (1 Corinthians 13:8). This is true *only* if God has a hand in building and maintaining that relationship.

Take a close look at the "loves" you've seen fail. What happened to commitment? Where were God's ideals? Was there enough forgiveness? I believe you'll discover great gaps in the relationships you review; rips that allowed sin, selfishness, and pride to flood in, destroying the final spark of something that was supposed to last forever.

It's true. Love never fails. But people do. I don't want you to be one of them. I want you to live a life filled with the love God created for us. It's worth standing up for, sacrificing for, forgiving for. Love can survive years of disappointments, nights of sadness, and days of toil. When two people are in love God's way, all the powers of Satan cannot bring them down.

So, how do you know you're in love? Compare your feelings and emotions to 1 Corinthians 13. Print that chapter out and post it on your wall. Review it verse by verse, item by item. If everything matches or at least is solidly heading in that direction, congratulations—you're in love!

PART 6

LIVING WELL *in a* SICK WORLD

Eight powerful habits of healthy people

Consequences

So, how do I talk healthy living to a bunch of anything-goes teenagers who've discovered that they can eat whatever they want, sleep as little as they please, party at full tilt for hours, slam their bodies into stationary objects without major injury (search for "Fails" on YouTube), and enjoy behaviors that everyone else says are dangerous yet don't seem to faze them in the slightest? What can I possibly say to you that will convince you to pay a little more attention to how you feed, rest, maintain, and otherwise treat your bulletproof self?

One word. *Consequences.*

Like it or not, out here in the wild, everything you do—both good and bad—comes with consequences attached. Oh, you may not discover them until years later, but trust me, you will.

Part of my life work has been to talk with really smart people. I've hosted radio and television programs on a wide variety of topics. A favorite with audiences is the subject of health. Everyone wants to bypass illness, pain, and early death if at all possible. (They also want to bypass bypasses.) So, I've had the privilege of hanging out with the rock stars of the health and wellness field.

I also enjoyed serving as editor of *Vibrant Life* magazine, the premier health journal of the Seventh-day Adventist Church.

Through thousands of interviews and articles, I discovered that modern science, combined with a working knowledge of Scripture and a good dose of learning from life experiences, can teach us a thing or two about gaining and maintaining optimum health.

Before we go any further, I need to clarify something. What I'm presenting in this section of the book helps you reach, as I said, *optimum* health, not *perfect* health. Big difference.

Perfection was one of the first casualties of Adam and Eve's sin. When they inserted evil into their lives and, by doing so, created the wild, God's perfect creation was altered in many profound ways. Perfection became an impossible dream for all of humankind. That said, even in a world gone wrong, there are *optimum* levels of health that can be reached—and they vary from person to person. Genetics plays a role too. So, your optimum level may be different from mine.

So, when I say that you can be healthy, I'm not saying that you can be perfect. Sorry, but that's not possible. However, by following these eight powerful habits, you can reach your own personal, *optimum level* of health, which may be far higher than what you would experience if you hadn't followed them.

Got that? OK. Let's continue.

During my journey through the wild, I've learned that most of today's chronic illnesses—many of which end in death—are generated by personal habits that are easily changed. I'm talking heart disease, diabetes, and even some forms of cancer! Life may load the gun, but we pull the trigger with how we treat our bodies. Yes, my friends, *there are consequences.* And they will let themselves be known somewhere, sometime, *every* time.

As we continue our journey, just know that what you do (or don't do) when it comes to health leaves a mark. But it may be a few years or even decades before you notice the scarring.

The good news is that you can minimize the potential damage at any time along the way, and believe me, you'll be glad you did.

I'll be speaking in broad terms. This isn't a health course. Think of it as a health *introduction.* You can uncover more amazing details as you study these topics for yourself moving forward.

But, for now, let's scratch the surface to see what we find out about the eight powerful habits of healthy people.

* * * * *

Habit 1—Insisting on Good Nutrition

Imagine this. You walk onto an airplane. The pilot takes you to ten thousand feet, and after you've leveled off, you stand in the doorway, looking down at the earth and admiring the clouds, rivers, farms, and all those tiny towns.

Then, you jump.

The wind races past your face. You sense movement by noticing that things below are beginning to get bigger as you enjoy the absolute freedom of drifting unattached and unencumbered. You're in what's called free fall, and adrenaline junkies everywhere can't seem to get enough of that amazing sensation. This part of the experience requires only one thing: an airplane. The joy, exhilaration, racing wind, and stunning views are included at no extra cost.

The next step—especially if you'd like a repeat performance—demands one added expense: a parachute. Without that second financial commitment, your exhilarating free fall would end badly.

I'm reminded of a Bible text I learned years ago: "There is a way that appears to be right, but in the end it leads to death" (Proverbs 14:12). It may seem right to enjoy all those thrills without the burden of carrying a parachute aloft. Whether you have one strapped to your back or not, the racing wind, amazing views, and joy of falling through the misty blue remain. It's the *outcome* that changes when you include a parachute as part of your adventure package.

I can think of no other arena of life where this Bible text fits more perfectly than in the often confusing world of health and nutrition.

I see many individuals, young and old, happily hopping on board the vegan, lacto-ovo vegetarian, raw, high-carb, low-carb, organic, humanely grown, high-protein, low-protein, no-sugar, high-fat, or no-fat express. They sometimes experience the joys of newfound energy, the reduction of many disease symptoms, and even the rush of feel-good hormones that spring to life when a body is energized by a simple change. They climb to new heights and then fling themselves out into space. They're in free fall and loving it.

The problem is that many of these individuals fail to include a parachute in their adventure, and the way that seems so right to them is about to end so wrong.

* * * * *

The Disease of Ignorance

No matter how you choose to live your life, an important point to keep in mind is that none of us are getting out of here alive. All our airy free falls terminate on the extremely solid planet Earth. Spending time gently swinging under a parachute both lengthens the thrill and eases us into the end of our adventure—a very different ending than slamming into the ground at terminal velocity. And there's something else to remember. Health shouldn't be only about living well. It should also be about dying well.

All too often, when I visit people who are in the hospital, I realize that what brought them there was ignorance concerning the care and feeding of their now-failing bodies. They bought into the concept that nutrition is guaranteed by marketing, that what the package says on their favorite foods is absolutely, unarguably true.

For instance, many of the "all-natural" processed products they've consumed for years contained a whole lot of "unnatural" carcinogens (substances that promote the development of cancer). If they'd been taught that—when it comes to food—the words *natural* and *healthy* should only describe *whole, unprocessed, plant* foods, they'd be much more likely to be gently swinging under a parachute right now instead of streaking earthward connected to a heart monitor, saline drip, and catheter.

Also, contrary to popular opinion, just because a food item is labeled "vegan" doesn't make it healthy. A meal consisting of a soft drink, potato chips, and doughnuts can be vegan. But it's certainly not healing to the mind or body. There is enough sugar, oil, and preservatives in that meal to cause an amazing amount of harm to the human anatomy. People who eat this way are falling and enjoying the rush. And they aren't wearing a parachute.

It's obvious that when people get sick, few of them stop to ask why. So many of us don't seem overly concerned as obesity rates and blood pressures rise, as type 2 diabetes turns epidemic, as hearts fail, and as minds become clouded with rage and memory loss. Everyone is happily in free fall, enjoying health-destroying taste sensations and overcoming daily stress with habits that further sap well-being and longevity. The ground is rushing up at them as they woefully blame their genes for their ailments.

"I need another pill," they tell their overworked doctors. "It's not my fault. Modern medicine can fix me anytime I want. I may have to have surgery, but then I'll be as good as new—"

Splat!

* * * * *

All or Nothing

Few realize or choose to accept that gaining and maintaining optimum health is very demanding. It doesn't allow you to moderate or cut back on what's hurting you. You can't just include a few good things. When it comes to health, it's all or nothing—kind of like a parachute. Either you have one, or you don't.

You can't *include* an item or two from a parachute and hope it will slow your descent—like, say, the rip cord and a few yards of ripstop fabric. Yet many believe that adding a few fruits and vegetables to their regular diet each day will heal the damage done by years of dietary free fall. Also, you can't *cut back* on the airplane's altitude in hopes that the fall won't be as deadly. Yet many *cut back* on their soda or meat intake, thinking they will make a sizable dent in their failing health. This decision can bring limited benefits, but it doesn't slow the tumble.

As for *moderation*, consider these telling words penned by Dr. Caldwell Esselstyn, an internationally known former surgeon, researcher, and clinician at the Cleveland Clinic. He writes:

> Moderation kills. . . .
>
> Every segment of our bodies is comprised of cells, and every individual cell is protected by an outer coat. . . .

> Every mouthful of oils and animal products, including dairy foods, initiates an assault on these membranes and, therefore, on the cells they protect. . . . Eventually, the cumulative cell injury is great enough to become obvious, to express itself as what physicians define as disease.*

Notice the name of the book from which that quote came: *Prevent and Reverse Heart Disease*. That's right—reverse! In fact, the word *reverse* is popping up more and more in health literature, such as in *Dr. Neal Barnard's Program for Reversing Diabetes*.

These medical scientists, and many others worldwide, are identifying the parachute we all need as we plummet toward our destination, enjoying the thrill of the fall. It's the one item that can slow our journey, making our lives longer, healthier, and more fulfilling. It's what may ease us into death without the usual months or years of pain and suffering. Under the billowing support of sound nutrition, we won't be living short and dying long, as is so often the case. We'll be enjoying life free of constant doctor visits, deadly drugs, dangerous lifestyle-altering surgeries, and the debilitating chronic illnesses that plague much of society.

That's exactly what I want for you.

* * * * *

Even Better

Believe it or not, the nutrition parachute does even more than *reverse* our diseases. It can help *prevent* them in the first place.

Epidemiologist T. Colin Campbell, the author of *The China Study*, sums it up nicely:

> The evidence now amassed from researchers around the world shows that the same diet that is good for the prevention of cancer is also good for the prevention of heart disease, as well as obesity, diabetes, cataracts, macular degeneration, Alzheimer's, cognitive dysfunction, multiple sclerosis, osteoporosis and other diseases. . . .
>
> . . . There is one diet to counteract all of these diseases: a whole foods, plant-based diet.†

---

* Caldwell B. Esselstyn Jr., *Prevent and Reverse Heart Disease* (New York: Avery, 2007), 38.

† T. Colin Campbell and Thomas M. Campbell II, *The China Study* (Dallas: BenBella Books, 2006), 109, 110.

And there it is.

To the Christian teenager, that revelation should sound familiar. On the seventh day of Creation week, as God walked and talked with Adam and Eve among the verdant avenues of Eden, everything necessary for optimum—and *eternal*—health was in place. Nothing was missing.

In your imagination, stand with Adam and Eve on that day and look around. What's there? Fresh air, clean water, an active lifestyle filled with outdoor, under-the-sun projects, companionship—both human and animal—a wonderful relationship with the Creator, and the very whole-food, plant-based diet that Dr. Campbell and his team of researchers discovered is so vital to our health.

My friend, here's the take-home message as we face life in the wild. The further we move away from that Eden ideal, the sicker we become. Conversely, the closer we live in harmony with God's original health plan, the more health we can enjoy now and down that long and winding road called life.

Barring an accident or other tragedy beyond our control, how we live now often determines how we die later. As well-known nutritionist and physician Dr. John McDougall told me during one of our many radio interviews, "It's the food, Charles. It's the food!"

We can either end our ride of life falling fast and out of control, or we can be gently swinging under that comforting parachute of disease prevention or reversal—all based on our lifestyle choices. It's as simple as that.

Yes, there is a way that seems right. But now we know the end from the beginning and can alter our experience, deciding both the length and quality of our free fall. We can choose our personal parachutes. That can make all the difference in how our journey ends.

* * * * *

Habit 2—Choosing Water

One day, decades ago in North Africa, a wireless message arrived from the vast regions of the Sahara Desert. The missive was short and to the point. Over and over again, the signal rattled radio receivers in every police headquarters for miles around. "Water," the single-word call repeated. "Water."

French authorities suspected it might have originated from three aviators who'd been missing for several days. They'd taken off on a long journey and never arrived at their destination. Everyone believed they were dead, swallowed whole by the endless expanse. Now, hope was renewed.

A search was quickly organized. Men and machines fanned out across the sands. Aircraft groaned into the air. Communication links were established, and soon a steady stream of information flowed back and forth between headquarters and personnel both on the ground and in the air.

After scouring thousands of miles of dry, barren land, the missing plane was spotted. Once safely rescued, the thankful flyers told how they'd managed to get their wireless working after much time and agonizing effort. By then, they were suffering from such a delirious thirst that all they could signal was that one repeated word—*water, water, water.*

There's a reason for that. Every single process in our bodies takes place in a bed of water. Cell division and growth, digestion, blood formation and cleaning, oxygen processing, and even the very act of thinking require water. Fun fact: our bodies are about 70 percent water. This colorless, tasteless, calorie- and salt-free substance is to our bodies what oil is to a car engine. It's the magic lubricant that makes everything work.

Knowing this, we humans must be consuming all the water we need, right? Wrong! Kids and teenagers are drowning in soft drinks instead. As they age, they add copious amounts of tea, coffee, and other beverages. Some mix in alcohol and "power" drinks without considering what's happening inside their water-starved selves.

What's happening is alarming. Every bodily process is being affected negatively—similar to what would happen if you tried to run your car without oil.

I'll let you use your imagination, but I'll get you started. Making the body work with limited amounts of H_2O is like trying to wash dishes in a cupful of liquid. When you don't drink enough water, your body must excrete wastes (leftovers from the very process of staying alive) in more concentrated forms, causing body odor, bad breath, and unpleasant-smelling urine.

Plus, you can't think as clearly, process your food as effectively, deal with elimination properly, or perform at your *optimum* levels (there's that word again). And no, soft drinks, tea, coffee, and other beverages can't do what water does. They have too much other stuff that irritates the delicate linings of the stomach and pushes the liver and kidneys into detoxifying and waste-disposing overdrive. They do more harm than good.

Bottom line: water is king!

By the way, that whole-food, plant-based diet I talked about at the beginning of this section? Whole plants comprise anywhere from 70 to 90 percent water. Seems the Creator knew what we needed even before we did.

Think about this the next time you're thirsty.

* * * * *

Habit 3 – Moving It

Healthy people move . . . a lot! They even get creative so that they can move even more than they normally would have to.

They park their cars at the far end of the parking lot when going shopping. They bypass the elevator and take the stairs whenever possible. If they work at sit-down jobs, they stand up and walk around their office or hike the hall for a sip of water at the drinking fountain at least every hour. I've known some who always stand up whenever they're talking on the phone.

Even their hobbies reflect their desire to move. Healthy people mountain bike, hike, jog, tend a vegetable garden, watch birds, or challenge themselves with landscape or nature photography. They canoe, swim, climb mountains, jump on mini trampolines, and basically keep their muscles active by doing anything but sitting still.

I'm a writer. That's the epitome of a not-moving profession (unless you call wiggling your figures exercise). I have to consciously tell myself to get up and move—go for a long walk, ride my bike somewhere, do yard work, whatever—just move.

The reason that moving is so important to the human body has been outlined in a book by Dr. Hans Diehl, founder of the Complete Health Improvement Program. I'm going to use him as an important source of information throughout the rest of this section of the book.

Here's a short list of why you need to keep moving. In his book *Health Power*, Dr. Diehl explains the benefits of exercise:

- Exercise helps us feel good. When we exercise, our bodies produce certain hormones that not only improve our health but also improve our mental outlook.
- Exercise strengthens the heart. Heart disease is a killer. Exercise is a killer of a killer.
- Exercise lowers blood pressure, reducing the strain on the vascular system.
- Exercise lowers LDL cholesterol levels. LDL cholesterol, also known as the bad cholesterol, contributes to plaque buildup in the arteries. (Yes, that's as bad as it sounds.)
- Exercise strengthens bones by helping them retain calcium and other vital minerals. Here's a perfect example of delayed consequences. You don't want to enter old age with weakened bones.

- Exercise lifts depression. I know this to be true. When life gets me down, a nice brisk walk is better than any drug. Even the side effects of walking are healthy: weight control and muscle toning.
- Exercise relieves anxiety and stress. Welcome to college. You've been warned.
- Exercise increases overall energy and efficiency. See previous.
- Exercise helps maintain desirable weight levels. Look around. Seems to me that not enough people—young or old—are moving enough.
- Exercise improves circulation. Better circulation creates clearer minds, better sleep, and faster healing of damaged body areas.*

So, why not start right now? Put the book down until later and form a plan for keeping active. Your health today—and down the road—depends on it.

* * * * *

Habit 4—Spending Time in the Sun

"Oh, I don't want to get skin cancer!" Ever heard anyone say that as they lathered themselves up with sunblock, jammed a wide-brimmed hat over their head, and headed for the beach dressed like an astronaut walking on the moon?

Actually, they have a point. *Excessive* exposure to sunlight can cause skin cancer, to say nothing of premature wrinkling and aging of our largest organ. But this fear has created another serious problem: *underexposure* to sunlight.

According to Dr. Diehl, harnessing the power of sunlight is vital to good health. That's why healthy people make a habit of catching the right amount of rays at the right time.

Ready for another list of benefits? Here goes:

- Sunlight helps regulate the production of melatonin, a natural hormone found to enhance sleep. Melatonin production is regulated by the light-dark cycle. Daily exposure to natural sunlight will boost melatonin output when it's dark. You heard me right. For a good night, you need to have a bright day.
- Sunlight kills germs. Word to the wise: the same sunlight that does a number on germs hiding in your skin also kills them on blankets, quilts, and other sleep items not washed regularly.

---

* Hans Diehl and Aileen Ludington, *Health Power* (Hagerstown, MD: Review and Herald®, 2011), 187.

- The proper amount of sunlight gives your skin a healthy glow and makes it smooth and pliable.
- Sunlight boosts your mood. Need an antidepressant? Walk outdoors in the fresh air and sunlight. Even during cold and gloomy months, catch as many rays as you can.
- Sunlight works with your body to produce vitamin D. Books have been written on the benefits of this vitamin and its incredible power to boost the immune system. (Hint: your bones and teeth will thank you too.)
- Sunlight does more. Besides that bump in immune system effectiveness, sunlight helps alleviate pain from swollen arthritic joints, relieves certain symptoms of PMS, and lowers blood cholesterol levels. Also, people who enjoy abundant sunshine are less likely to suffer from breast, colon, or prostate cancer.*

Keep the following recommendations in mind: Modest tanning is protective. Burning the skin is bad, very bad. Try to get a minimum of ten to fifteen minutes of sun exposure to your arms and face per day. Most people will benefit from thirty minutes of sunshine. After that, wear protective clothing, eyewear, and sunscreen when needed.

Enjoy your day in the sun!

* * * * *

Habit 5—Have a Certain Air About You

You may find this hard to believe, but many people don't get enough air. The stuff is available most anywhere we go, yet we suffer from a lack of it. How is that possible?

Here's how.

We've learned that water is the lubrication of the human body. Well, air is the spark that ignites the fuel (nutrition) that we provide the body. Without water or air, we die. But two things are happening in the world these days: our air is dirty, and our breathing habits inhibit proper air intake. Lose-lose.

According to Dr. Diehl, these two realities can promote negative emotions and cause headaches and chronic feelings of exhaustion.

Cleaning up the air we breathe may be as simple as staying away from where the air is dirty—like in cities and near factories. But, if we need to live where the

* Diehl and Ludington, *Health Power*, 194, 195.

air is not clean, we'd better have a lot of houseplants in our homes and maybe an air purifier running in the background. Also, spending time in nature breathing unpolluted air does wonders for our health. Scientists say that air containing lots of negative ions is best. Where do we find those? Around lakes, in forests, near rivers and waterfalls, at the seashore, and right after a rainstorm.

When it comes to breathing correctly, here are some suggestions:

- Don't slouch when you're sitting. Keep that back straight and shoulders squared. Now your lungs have room to operate.
- If you discover that your breathing tends to be shallow, consciously start breathing more deeply.
- If the clothes you're wearing restrict your breathing, go a little looser.
- Open the windows in your bedroom or office. Stuffy isn't good.
- Exercise enough to get you breathing more rapidly for a few minutes every day.
- You know that high-fat meal you just ate (animal products or other foods with a high oil content)? Fat and oil reduce your blood's ability to carry oxygen. You may be suffocating yourself from the inside out! Choose whole plant foods instead. Most have very little fat. They can help you breathe better.
- Don't just sit there. Move! Get up, walk around, and draw in some deep, cleansing breaths.*

God provided our original breath of life. We can keep it refreshed by following these simple, life-lengthening guidelines.

* * * * *

Habit 6—Catching Z's

I've known some teenagers who were proud of how little sleep they got. "Hey, I caught just about two hours last night, and I feel great," they say. "Sleep? Who needs it? That's for old people and babies." "I've got too much to do! I can't waste my life sleeping."

Reality check: While your youth may hide it from you for a time, lack of sleep robs you down the road. Proper sleep is vital to your health and longevity. Remember those consequences we talked about?

* Diehl and Ludington, *Health Power*, 202–205.

In today's full-on lifestyle, people are choking down millions of sedatives and tranquilizers each day, desperate for rest. They're always tired, complaining about chronic fatigue and wondering why they can't think straight.

One cardiologist suggests that the electric light bulb is the reason for the problem. And he has a point. People used to go to bed when it got dark outside, following their built-in circadian rhythm (a natural, internal process that regulates the sleep-wake cycle based on the rotation of the earth). Then along came Thomas Edison and his "artificial sunlight." Suddenly, there's no night. Only endless day. Who needs a circadian rhythm?

Seems your body does.

Dr. Diehl says it's not only how *much* you sleep but *when* and how *regularly* it happens. He reports that the average sleep time in the last century has declined 20 percent. He also says that teenagers need an average of nine hours of dream time per night, but most don't even come close to that. This may contribute to this sad statistic. The National Transportation Safety Board estimates that 100,000 police-reported car crashes by drowsy drivers cause up to 1,550 deaths and 71,000 injuries each year.*

Consequences.

So, how can you sleep better? Consider these time-proven suggestions:

- Take frequent breaks during your work or school day. And don't forget to move, breathe deeply, and hydrate yourself with plain, simple water.
- Exercise thirty to sixty minutes each day. This should not be a problem for most teenagers—at least the ones I know.
- Go to bed, get up, eat, and exercise on a regular schedule. Your body loves rhythms.
- Eat your last meal of the day at least four hours before bedtime. An empty stomach promotes quality rest.
- Try a lukewarm bath to relax. Not hot. Certainly not cold. Lukewarm.
- Fill your mind with gratitude and thanksgiving for the blessings you enjoy. This is one of my favorite ways to relax.
- Remember, a clear, uncluttered conscience makes a wonderful pillow on which to sleep.†

Good night!

* * * * *

* Taylor Covington, "Drowsy Driving Statistics," The Zebra, updated September 30, 2021, https://www.thezebra.com/resources/research/drowsy-driving-statistics/.

† Diehl and Ludington, *Health Power*, 207, 208.

Habit 7—Don't Overdo It

Full disclosure. I'm a workaholic. Always have been. If I'm not working on a project, I'm thinking about it, planning it, or worrying about it. I tend to overdo everything, and that's not good. But I'm better than I used to be. I guess I've lived long enough to recognize the consequences of such chronic insanity.

Of course, I've known people who are the polar opposite. They seem to flow through life in a relaxed state, just getting by, doing just enough, and seldom giving 100 percent to anything.

Optimum health requires something in the middle. You do your best with diligence, passion, and commitment. You give that 100 percent—but in controlled bursts. And you don't overdo, causing yourself added stress and pressure.

It's the same in all areas of life. Healthy people have learned a sense of balance, and they apply that balance to work, play, worship, concern, and joy.

Teenagers tend to do *everything* to excess—must be the hormones. They often eat, drink, spend, and party far too hardy. These things aren't necessarily bad. They just need to be balanced with commonsense habits that include sound nutrition, sufficient exercise, much-needed rest, and a genuine concern for their well-being and the well-being of others.

To me, there's not a more powerful force for good in this world than an energetic teenager with a concern for others. I've seen them in action, and it's incredible what they can accomplish when they're living in balance with nature and the needs of the human body. I praise God for their self-regulated drive and stamina.

I once wrote a song for a health project that included these lyrics in the chorus:

Don't overdo wha'cha do, wha'cha do.
Don't overdo wha'cha do.
You like to play? Well, that's OK.
Just don't overdo wha'cha do.

Think about the tortoise and its race with the rabbit. The bunny is all about speed but often wears itself out and is forced to stop from exhaustion. The tortoise, on the other hand, has learned how to incorporate rest with movement and can keep going and going and going—eventually, according to the story, crossing the finish line first.

Be the tortoise.

* * * * *

Habit 8—Trust in a Benevolent Power

For the Christian, this last habit of highly healthy people is vital. Notice I used the term "*benevolent* power."

Section 2 of this book identified when the real God—the God of love—became "fake news" in the minds of humankind. He stopped being the prime example of love and acceptance and became the prime example of fear and rejection. Satan served as the headmaster in that university of sin.

But then, something happened. Jesus came to this sin-filled world to reintroduce the Father—the real Father, the loving Father. And He paid for that privilege with His life.

Placing our trust in a benevolent (well-meaning, kind, tender, forgiving, loving) power has a far different effect on our health than bowing to that raging, destroying, condemning, judgmental power we hear about from many church pulpits these days.

It's common knowledge that we tend to become like what we worship, and while benevolence has a calming, healing impact on us, all that judging and condemning destroys us from the inside out. Remember, we were created to love. When we're doing anything but loving, we're operating outside of our original design specs—kind of like driving a car over a cliff and hoping it will fly.

So, while trusting in a divine power is essential to our well-being, what or whom we're trusting makes a huge difference in how much that habit impacts our overall health. The good news is that learning to trust in the *real* God—the *Jesus* God, the God of love, acceptance, and forgiveness—alters our mind, body, and spirit in profound and positive ways.

Have you ever met someone who, in the past, was a royal pain? His or her life seemed to revolve around them. They were unkind, unmoving, and unforgiving. Then they met Jesus, the kind One, the passionate One, the forgiving One. And their life was changed. They began to reflect God's love in ways you'd never seen before. That's what I'm talking about.

So, my friend, worship is important. Trust is important. Please allow Jesus to introduce you to your Father in heaven. Allow Him to set the record straight by showing you the truth through His life and teaching. Believe me, your mind, body, and spirit will respond in healing and healthy ways.

* * * * *

The Real God

With your permission, I'd like to end this section on healthy living by presenting a story that appeared in another book I wrote called *Religion in the Real World*.* *This* is the God I invite you to worship. *This* is the God I want you to imagine when you bow to pray. This is the *real* God—the One who made you, the One who can rebuild you, body and soul, if you're willing. His love is the best medicine on earth.

If you want to be healthy—truly healthy—get to know this Jesus. He alone can heal you from the inside out.

I call the story "The View from the Cross,"† and I hope you enjoy it.

It was warm the afternoon I stood below the hill where Jesus died.

Like every other "holy" patch of real estate in and around Jerusalem, Gordon's Calvary is simply a best guess for the actual location of the Crucifixion. But it does seem to fit the requirements outlined in the Bible. The Jews call it Beth-has-sekilah, or "house of stoning," where early Christian tradition places the martyrdom of Stephen. In other words, this fifty-foot, rocky precipice just outside the Damascus Gate of the northwest wall of the city was where bad guys went to be executed. The fact that its jagged shape bears an uncanny resemblance to a skull only heightens its believability.

But I wasn't looking for archeological proof of anything that day. I was looking for Jesus. What I found altered my perception of Him, not only because of what happened there but because of something He said. That particular utterance went unmentioned by three of the four Gospel writers. Only Dr. Luke bothered to write it down, and I'm so glad he did.

We as practicing Christians are often instructed to "go to the foot of the cross" to learn about God's love. We're invited to gaze up at the dying Savior to determine our worth, to realize our eternal potential, and to find the hope for which we all desperately long. But what if our view changed? What if we were no longer at the foot of the cross looking up but hanging from it looking down? We'd be seeing what Jesus saw as the life slowly drained from His body that fateful Friday afternoon. Suddenly, the words He managed to move past swollen, bloody lips take on a whole new meaning, especially the one particular phrase that Luke included in his Gospel.

The view from the cross of Calvary encompassed much more than the

* Charles Mills, *Religion in the Real World* (Nampa, ID: Pacific Press®, 2019).

† Mills, *Religion in the Real World*, 57–60.

jagged hilltop. It included the upturned faces of those who'd come to watch Him die and those who'd put Him there. In His field of vision, Jesus could see the busy road leading to and from the Damascus Gate with its surging crowds, the powerful and proud stone walls encircling the city, the tall spires of Jerusalem, and the shimmering ramparts of the temple. Beyond flowed the undulating dry and barren hills of Judea, where occasional flocks of sheep wandered among the rocks and thorns. On Calvary's hill, there's much to see when you're being crucified.

This brings us to those amazing words found in chapter 23 of the Gospel of Luke. After the good doctor had described in detail the arrest, mock trial, and subsequent condemnation of Christ, his report carries us to "the place called the Skull," where Jesus was crucified (verse 33). Luke mentioned that "two other men, both criminals, were also led out with him to be executed" (verse 32).

Now we find Jesus nailed to a Roman cross, with two bad guys, one on each side, hanging from crosses of their own. I'm guessing the efficient Romans decided that as long as the execution squad was up and running that day, they may as well clean out the local lockup's death row.

That's when it happened. "Jesus said, 'Father, forgive them, for they do not know what they are doing' " (verse 34).

Mockers and murderers

Forgive whom? The bad guys? The soldiers still gripping their blood-stained hammers? The self-absorbed spiritual rulers who'd arranged to have Jesus put on the cross and were, even at that moment, calling out, "He saved others; let him save himself if he is God's Messiah, the Chosen One" (verse 35)? Was He forgiving the disciples who, just the night before, had disowned Him? Perhaps it was the numb onlookers who couldn't care less about who was dying outside the city walls and were there simply out of morbid curiosity.

Luke doesn't say, but the view from the cross included every one of those individuals. Christ's vantage point also encompassed the masses of people moving in and out of the city through the Damascus Gate, the merchants and their customers filling the busy streets of Jerusalem, the priests going about their solemn duties in the temple, and the lowly shepherds keeping watch over their flocks among the parched hills of Judea.

I believe those agonizing words, "Father, forgive them," reveal the true character of Christ. They highlight a personality trait that proves beyond a doubt that, even while dying a horrible death, His thoughts were not on Himself but on others.

Luke must have concluded that those particular words would mean something important to future generations of sinners, including us. In that sweeping view from the cross, we can surely find ourselves.

Perhaps our actions have condemned the Savior anew. Maybe we've disowned Him, calling Him irrelevant for life in the twenty-first century. Our callous ways have been spikes driven through His hands and feet. We've banned His message of love and forgiveness from our churches, spending precious worship time arguing politics or defending sinful ways using vague references straight from the Bible. We've rejected Him in public, choosing to be "cool" or "worldly" instead of sticking to what we know to be right.

For many of us, finding no divine support for our lifestyle, we simply ignore God's presence in our lives. We go about our business without a glance in His direction. His sacrifice means nothing. After all, we have problems of our own to face and fail to see how a dying Jewish rabbi could impact life's outcomes.

Finally, we roam the barren hills alone, failing to accept the companionship of a God who understands us much more than we realize.

Hidden message

But hidden within those words, we discover a special brand of hope for all people. Jesus provided an astonishing insight into what motivates God's forgiving spirit, even when it comes to sinners like us. The dying Savior cried out, "Father, forgive them, *for they do not know what they are doing*" (verse 34; emphasis added).

If we've reached a self-destructive point in our lives because of sin-enhanced ignorance, the full weight of God's forgiveness is waiting to be applied. We also need to know that Satan has an uncanny way of making wrong seem right and right seem unimportant. Our minds, saturated with evil, willingly accept the devil's substitute spirituality, and in doing so, we set ourselves up to live our lives unconcerned and unmotivated by things of true value.

Jesus understood this. When He looked down on the callous Roman soldiers, the angry religious persecutors, the fear-driven disciples, and the curious mobs hurling insults at Him, He understood their total ignorance.

How could He condemn what they were doing when *they* didn't understand what they were doing? How could He call down vengeance on people who were under the direct influence of power far stronger than they could comprehend? He couldn't. And He didn't. Instead, His words recorded by Luke reveal a fathomless love that overlooks actions and offers hope to anyone willing to change allegiance and start living a life motivated by eternal values instead of worldly emotions.

Those words still echo today. God's forgiveness remains readily accessible. It doesn't matter if, in His view from the cross, we're represented by the soldiers, the disciples, the throngs of people, the merchants and sellers, the spiritual leaders, or the man or woman wandering alone among barren hills. It's time for us to trade ignorance for enlightenment and experience God's brand of forgiveness and hope.

Don't take my word for it. Listen to what Simon Peter—a disciple who had disowned Christ the night of His trial and stood in the shadows of the cross watching the Savior die—later wrote to members of the early Christian church: "But you are a chosen people, a royal priesthood, a holy nation, God's special possession, that you may declare the praises of him who called you out of darkness into his wonderful light. Once you were not a people, but now you are the people of God; once you had not received mercy, but now you have received mercy" (1 Peter 2:9, 10).

A hill far away

My father, missionary Robert C. Mills, once visited that same rugged hilltop years ago. He spoke of standing among the Muslim tombs that now dot the site of Gordon's Calvary and watching the city of Jerusalem bask in the late afternoon light. He saw the cars and trucks passing by below as throngs of people moved in and out of the Damascus Gate. He heard the buses arriving and departing the bus station located at the foot of the hill. Like me, he allowed the memories of what happened there two thousand years ago to dominate his thoughts.

He told me later that he found himself humming a familiar hymn: "On a hill far away stood an old rugged cross."* Then he suddenly realized that the hill wasn't far away at all. It was right there under his feet.

With tears, he added, "Instantly, another old, favorite song from my childhood sprang to mind. How thrilling it will be when the 'sweet by and by'† is today."

Thanks to those incredible words uttered by Christ on a place called the Skull, we know that millions—including each one of us—can accept that healing forgiveness and look forward to an eternal life free from disease and pain, all because of what Christ saw from the cross.

* George Bennard, "The Old Rugged Cross," 1913.
† Sanford Fillmore Bennett, "In the Sweet By and By," 1868.

PART 7

PREPARING *for* PARADISE

Begin your heavenward journey today.

Painting God's Portrait

Then God said, "Let us make mankind in our image, in our likeness."
—Genesis 1:26

This final section of the book is designed to provide you with some food for thought. You can apply the lessons I present any way you wish as you make your way through the wild toward heaven. I may not know you personally. I may not see the exact challenges you face, but we're on this journey together, and I want to give you something to think about along the way.

So, instead of saying, "Do this," or, "Do that," I'm going to sit back and share some insights and adventures that have proven helpful to me. I'm hoping they'll do the same for you. We're all different. But we worship the same God—the Creator God, the God who loves us and works tirelessly to save us. What He has taught me through the years may be exactly what He's hoping to teach you. All I'm asking is that you be open to His still, small voice as you read.

You may not know this, but you're an artist. We all are! We all must paint our own portrait of who God is and how God acts. Just how that image is formed may require many sources. I want to be one of those sources for you.

When I was a little boy, a friend told me that God lived in the clouds. Every time a storm rumbled across the sky, I thought my heavenly Father was angry at me, so I'd run and hide.

Then I was told He lives in my body. Every time I did something foolish, I figured God must be on vacation. When I was good, I'd glance in the mirror and think, *Is that God looking back at me now?*

Today, I know better. God lives in both the clouds and my heart. And I've learned to appreciate His constant presence in my life.

I've also learned what it takes to paint a true picture of our heavenly Father for the world to see. Here's what I've concluded.

First, we must have a clean, white canvas because God is sinless and perfect. Our easel must be strong, for God is our foundation. We must purchase the best pigments because God always provides what's best for us. Our brushes must be made from the finest materials, for God can be painted only from the purity of thought and action.

We begin by sketching an outline of our hopes and dreams. Subtle shadows of doubt must be smoothed into the bold lines of victory. This forms the background of our masterpiece.

The face of Christ appears next. We trace the eyes that lovingly watch our every move, the ears that hear our every cry, and the lips that speak words only we can hear. We form the hands that felt the nails, the feet that run to our aid, and the arms longing to hold us.

If our paints dry, we wet them with our tears. This makes the colors brighter.

Finally, we frame our picture using rough, timeworn wood from the cross.

After hanging our masterpiece in our hearts, we notice a lone figure standing before it. He looks intently at the colors and studies every line. Then He smiles. "Well done," He says. "Enter now into the joy of your Lord."

With thanksgiving, we bow and worship at the feet of the Creator. We're truly revealing His image—and His character—to the world.

* * * * *

The Mother in Our Father

This is love: not that we loved God, but that he loved us.

—1 John 4:10

The living room clock chimes twice. I lie facing the window, staring out at the star-littered sky. My mother sleeps in the chair by my bed, her hand holding mine, her head resting against my knee.

She came in hours ago to stroke my forehead. Her gentle touch always eased the uncertainty of sickness. I close my eyes and drift to sleep, knowing my mother will keep her silent vigil over me.

Mother love. No count of miles, no passing of years can outdistance the bond between a loving mother and her child. As the world consumes itself with hate, mother love often remains the one clear light illuminating a multitude of lives.

We speak of God as "our Father." But I think there's more to be said about Him. Long ago, He took a very special part of Himself and molded it into a being called mother. Each mother's touch is His touch; each tear, His tear.

A group of shepherds crowded around a wooden manger as a woman gently smoothed the rough blanket placed about her newborn son. "Hush, little Jesus, don't cry," she whispers. "Your Father and I are watching over You."

In our imagination, we see another scene. This same mother stands at the foot of a Roman cross. Above her, suspended by nails, the baby, now grown, hangs limp and lifeless. The woman doesn't move, eyes gazing at the still profile of her Son. Her lips form a phrase too agonizing to utter aloud. "Hush, little Jesus," she breathes, "don't cry. Your Father and I are watching over You."

Out here in the wild, we're all children of God. The love of earthly fathers and mothers represents a weak but noble reflection of Heaven's affection for us. But we can always feel safe and secure resting in the everlasting arms of our Creator. When our hearts feel fear and our eyes fill with tears, we will hear Him saying to us, "Hush, my child, don't cry. Your Father and I are watching over you."

* * * * *

How You Can Know God's Will for Your Life—Part 1

"For I have come down from heaven not to do my will but to do the will of him who sent me."

—John 6:38

Insha'Allah. This is a common utterance throughout the Middle East, where I used to live.* It means, "If it is God's will." You hear it all the time. "I'll leave on my business trip tomorrow, Insha'Allah." "I'll make it safely home, Insha'Allah." "I'm getting married next week, Insha'Allah." "My child will get well, Insha'Allah." Seems that in the mind of many Arabs, most, if not all, events are connected to the will of God.

This thinking is also embedded in the minds of countless Christians worldwide. "God led me to this job (or this person, or this lifestyle)." "Everything happens for a reason." "There are no accidents." "God has a special someone waiting just for me."

One devoutly spiritual woman told me that when she opens her refrigerator door each morning, she asks God what she should fix her husband for breakfast. Apparently, He tells her. He also instructs her on what to wear and what projects to include in her busy schedule. For some people, *everything* that happens is God's will.

Years ago, my nephew's son slipped and hit his head on the edge of a table while playing at a fast-food restaurant. The injury caused dangerous swelling inside his skull, and within hours, he was at a children's hospital having part of his brain removed in order to save his life. Well-meaning church members assured the child's terrified parents that "God's ways are mysterious. Right now, we don't understand why this happened, but someday we will. It's all part of His plan."

Part of God's plan? Really?

The truth is, God had nothing to do with the tragedy. That precious little boy

---

* This content previously published as Charles Mills, "How Can You Know God's Will for Your Life?" *Signs of the Times*, October 2018, 45, 46.

was the victim of slippery surfaces and gravity. Inferring that God orchestrated the accident was, in my estimation, a spiritual felony. Praise God, my great-nephew survived and recently graduated from college!

When a loved one lies at death's door, friends and family often plead for healing but leave the door open. "Thy will be done," they pray through their tears. Then, if the person lives, it's a "miracle." If he or she dies, God "laid him to rest" or "took her home to be with Him" (depending on their view of what happens after death).

Is God really that involved in our lives—in the nitty-gritty of our day-to-day existence? Is there some divine plan we need to be following, and if we don't, we pay a terrible price? The short answer is yes. But exactly *how* this plan is revealed and accomplished is what's important to know.

* * * * *

How You Can Know God's Will for Your Life—Part 2

Do not conform to the pattern of this world, but be transformed by the renewing of your mind. Then you will be able to test and approve what God's will is—his good, pleasing and perfect will.

—Romans 12:2

As with all things that have to do with our heavenly Father, it's best to search Scripture for answers.* The apostle Paul addressed the issue of what God's will actually is three times.

First, it's important to realize that God's will is not usually discovered through human, sin-clouded thinking. Why? Because we're often tempted to bend what we believe is God's will to our desires. If we can convince ourselves that what we want to do is ordained by God, we can feel free to "step out in faith," often to our disappointment or even destruction. I've seen this happen in various Christian ministries through the years. They follow God's "will" straight to bankruptcy.

The problem is that when the marriage, the job, or the journey fails miserably, we begin to question our heavenly Father's leading. *God steered us wrong*, we think. Bitterness and loss of faith often follow.

In his letter to the Thessalonians, Paul shines a bright light on what God's will

* Mills, "How Can You Know God's Will for Your Life?" *Signs of the Times*, October 2018, 46–48.

actually is—and his revelation may shock some people. Here it is: "It is God's will that you should be sanctified: that you should avoid sexual immorality" (1 Thessalonians 4:3). A few verses later, he adds: "Give thanks in all circumstances; for this is God's will for you in Christ Jesus" (1 Thessalonians 5:18).

So, God's will—as identified by Paul—is that we stop sinning, remain moral, and be thankful for our blessings.

Other New Testament writers provide further insights. Peter reveals that God wants us to do good so we can silence ignorant or foolish people (1 Peter 2:15). John reminds us that when we build our lives within the framework of God's will, we will outlast the world (1 John 2:17).

Where's the grand plan?

What we *don't* find in the Bible is the concept that God's will is anything but an overarching desire expressed by our heavenly Father that we live a victorious life. Where's the nitty-gritty? Where's the day-to-day guidance? Where's the grand plan? Oh, they're all there, but they're beautifully encased in something practical and easy to understand. God's will—His road map, His to-do list, His detailed outline for our lives—is fully revealed *in His words*. As Paul wrote, "All Scripture is God-breathed and is useful for teaching, rebuking, correcting and training in righteousness" (2 Timothy 3:16).

That means we can examine Scripture and discover His amazing and detailed health plan—including diet standards—as revealed in the Garden of Eden. This will guide our choices at the grocery store and when we're peering into our refrigerator.

Instead of praying for "the right one" to come along—the one God has "chosen" for us—we'd do well to make all our decisions based on the type of person God wants *us* to be. Then we will attract—and be attracted to—the type of life partner who will minimize potential conflicts down the road and maximize our chances for marital success.

Instead of trying to determine God's will in our career choices, why don't we first commit ourselves to a life of service to the One who loves us most and then make decisions based on the level of service opportunities each potential job provides.

Instead of trying to connect God to the bad things that happen to us or our families, why don't we turn to God for comfort and the power to rebuild when sin does its damage? The devil is thrilled when God gets blamed for the terrible things sin does.

Let God's Word be your guide. Then, when you pray, "Your will be done," you'll know what God's will really is.

*****

How You Can Know God's Will for Your Life—Part 3

"For my Father's will is that everyone who looks to the Son and believes in him shall have eternal life, and I will raise them up at the last day."
—John 6:40

God's "will" can be summed up with one word: *salvation*. Everything that happens may or may not be directly connected to that concept, but our *reaction* to everything that happens certainly is. We should ask, "Are my responses, my decisions, my choices supporting my journey to heaven?" If we can answer yes to those questions, we can rest assured that we are faithfully following God's will and can look forward to a future world where sin and sinners are no more.

Jesus said, "And this is the will of him who sent me, that I shall lose none of all those he has given me, but raise them up at the last day" (John 6:39).

In the earth made new, we can finally rest from our labors and know that we're there not only because God willed it but also because *we* did.

Want to know God's will for your life? Study His words, and then act accordingly.*

The following verses describe how the Bible identifies God's will in our lives and how we can live securely within His desires for us. Feel free to compare your life to this heavenly standard. If you fall short (as I certainly do from time to time), don't worry. God's will contains a whole lot of forgiveness baked right in.

OK. Here's how the Bible lays out God's will for us:

Romans 12:1, 2	Don't conform to the pattern of this world.
Galatians 1:4	Appreciate the fact that Christ rescued us from evil.
Ephesians 1:4	Be blameless.
Ephesians 1:11	Know we've been chosen for salvation.
	Understand our way to salvation already exists.
Ephesians 3:3–5	Comprehend the mystery of Christ.

* Mills, "How Can You Know God's Will for Your Life?" *Signs of the Times*, October 2018, 47, 48.

Ephesians 3:17	Enjoy the fact that we can be rooted and grounded in love.
Ephesians 5:1–17	Walk in the way of love.
	Do not be greedy.
	Avoid foolish talk or coarse joking.
	Live in the light of obedience.
	Don't be foolish.
Colossians 1:9–14	Gain understanding.
	Be thankful that we've been rescued from sin.
	Know our sins are forgiven.
Colossians 1:27	Have the hope of glory.
1 Thessalonians 4:3, 4	Avoid sexual immorality.
1 Thessalonians 5:9, 10	Know we weren't created to suffer wrath but to receive salvation.
1 Thessalonians 5:15–23	Strive to do what's good for everyone.
	Rejoice in all circumstances.
	Test prophecies and hold on to what is good.
	Reject every kind of evil.
1 Timothy 2:4	Come to a knowledge of the truth.
James 1:12	Know there's a crown waiting for us.
James 1:18	Realize that God ignited our spiritual growth.
James 1:27	Look after orphans and widows in their distress.
	We keep ourselves from being polluted by the world.
1 John 2:15–17	Do not love the world or anything in it.
	Praise God that we will live forever.
1 John 3:1	Rejoice that we are called "children of God."
1 John 5:13–16	Be glad that we have eternal life.
	Enjoy the confidence to approach God and ask for help.
	Always pray for others.

* * * * *

Mountains

And so, my friend, we now come to the last devotional of this book. Before I let you go, I want to thank you for spending a little time with me and, hopefully, catching a glimpse of what God can mean to you as you journey into the wild.

If you've made it to this page, I know that you're serious about living your life in service to the One who loves you, the One who wants to guide you and can save you from the evil that's all around us. If your heart has been touched by what has been presented here, just know that the Holy Spirit is hard at work in your life. You are not alone.

I leave you with words I wrote when I first started writing for teenagers. This is an article that appeared in the March 28, 1987, issue of *Insight* magazine, a weekly journal dedicated to the young people of that time who may have become your mother and father. It's my prayer that the thoughts I shared with them will reach deep into your heart and draw you closer to the God who made you. He's right nearby, waiting to lead you through every valley and help you conquer every mountain.

Journey in God's peace, my friend. And don't sweat the mountains.

The propeller spins invisibly. Tires roll over rough blacktop. Air sweeps past gently curved wings. My little yellow-and-white Citabria airplane strains to break gravity's hold as the ground becomes a moving ribbon of color. With a final bounce, the wood, metal, and fabric that forms my world lifts and points its nose into the clear sky.

Stick and rudder move together as we bank in a climbing turn over the Angwin, California, airport as the beautiful campus of Pacific Union College slips by. I work there as manager of their teaching radio station, KANG-FM.

I smile to myself. If everyone knew this feeling—this freedom—there'd be a line of people waiting outside the small flight school on the field. Never mind what it costs to learn; there'd be a line.

We climb eastward, my plane and I. Destination this day? Simply, to fly!

At 5,500 feet, we level off and glide serenely out over the Sacramento Valley.

Maybe it's just as well, I think to myself, listening to the roar of the engine. *Too many people up here would spoil the fun. But if they only knew what they were missing!*

It's a clear California day. Visibility reaches to infinity. Beyond the flat rice paddies of the valley rises the snowcapped Sierra Nevada range. A simple change of direction presents a panorama of sun and water as the Pacific Ocean laps over distant shores. This day was made for flying.

All at once, a certain sight catches the corner of my thoughts. There it is again, on the horizon. I bank right, my airplane rotating from sea to forest to farms. Far to the north, beyond the distant neck of the broad valley, stands Mount Shasta.

We fly, drawn by a magnetic emotion that mountains create in me. Slowly, Shasta grows as mile by mile we approach its kingdom of stone and snow. Occasionally, a stray cloud glides eastward from the sea. It rides the updrafts on the western slopes and passes over the summit, only to descend to its original height and then journey on.

Ridiculous

The thought seems ridiculous at first. I dismiss it as some childish fancy I'm supposed to have outgrown. But it returns with increasing intensity.

Fly over the mountain. Fly over the mountain!

"Can't be done," I say aloud to myself. "It's too high for my little airplane."

Fly over the mountain. Fly over the mountain.

"I said, it can't be done!" I feel intimidated by the impulse. "We can't fly that high."

The cloud did.

I lean forward against my seat belt and strain to see the winds flowing up and over the distant summit. Suddenly, I feel foolish. No one can see the wind.

You're a pilot. Feel the wind.

"Listen," I say, trying to bury the thought, "this airplane can't fly over the mountain, and that's final!"

The airplane can't? Or you can't?

I sit listening to the engine and the wind shrieking past my wings. In my hand, I feel the vibrations of flight. I move the control stick from side to side, guiding the craft closer and closer to the mountain. "What do you mean I can't?" I snarl, trying to control a wave of sudden anger. "I'm only as good as my airplane."

And it's only as good as you let it be, comes the silent reply. *How will you know how good your plane is until you make it do something really fantastic? Fly over the mountain!*

The face of Shasta coldly regards our approach. I gaze up toward the summit, looking for a reason to avoid the challenge. None appears. The mountain sits calm, uncaring, as we buzz by its rugged chin.

No one would believe me

"Look," I say, trying to sound mature and knowledgeable. "We *could* fly over the mountain, but why should we? What difference would it make to anyone?

No one would believe me even if we did."

High above, a passenger airliner tows a contrail north on its way to Seattle. Inside, people eat or snooze or gaze out the window enjoying the view. I can imagine a deep-throated captain pointing out the landmarks for those interested.

"On your right, the beautiful Sierra Nevada range. On your left, Mount Shasta. And, by the way, the pilot of that little yellow and white airplane puttering along down there is contemplating flying over the top of the mountain. Personally, I don't see what the big deal is: I do it twice a day on my way to and from Seattle. The fact that the airplane is not the same as mine should make no difference at all, especially if it's being flown by an intelligent pilot."

"Oh, sure!" I retort to the imagined remarks as the airliner glides toward the horizon. "That's easy for you say 'cause you're in a pressurized, jet-powered, autopiloted, multimillion-dollar airliner. My little mount is frail and fragile. I can't ask it to do out-of-the-ordinary things."

From the north comes the fading response. "An airplane is an airplane."

Suddenly, my Citabria jolts. I glance at the vertical speed indicator. We're climbing. We're climbing! An unseen river of air has caught my little craft in its current and is lifting it in an invisible, ascending stream just as it did the little cloud. Higher and higher we fly, riding this fast-moving elevator flowing up the mountain. I quickly adjust the engine's mixture control, trying to compensate for the rapidly thinning atmosphere.

My eyes see it, but I refuse to accept the sight. The summit, *the summit*! It's still far above but sliding toward us! We're going to fly right over the top of Mount Shasta. I don't believe it. We're going to—

The elevator ride slams to a stop. The airplane wallows in air made thin by the higher altitude. We've flown out of the river of air.

The engine tries to produce enough power to keep us at altitude, but the oxygen-starved atmosphere robs its strength. We're descending.

Just once?

I bank steeply, trying to move away from the mountain. The airplane responds sluggishly. We've lost. I was right. I shouldn't have even tried it.

Just once? You're going to give up after trying just once? The voice in my head sounds sullen.

"Look," I say, trying to control my disappointment. "Leave me alone! Don't you feel the way the airplane flies? It can't make it; the air is too thin!"

But the river. You didn't stay in the river. It's not the airplane's fault. It's your fault. It's not the mountain. It's not the engine. It's not the wings. It's you. You *can't fly over the top!*

"All right, all right!" I shout at the wind and noise and the voice in my head.

"It's me. I know it's me. I'm terrified of the mountain. There, I said it. Are you satisfied? I'm afraid to fly over the top of the mountain."

I wait for a response. None comes. My words hang in the cold air of my tiny, mechanical world.

The mountain provided the challenge; the rising air offered me the means; the plane was the vehicle. But I hadn't used the elements properly. Fear had made me careless. Fear had stolen my victory.

I feel a deep sadness. I've let the unknown conquer me again. I've turned away from a great personal accomplishment because I let fear steal the tools for success right out of my hands.

The airplane jolts. The river! I've stumbled into the rising flow of air once again. Shasta is giving me a second chance!

My mind stumbles with indecision. The mountain is so big, and I'm so small. I veer away.

The river, you had the river!

My airplane is so little, so fragile.

An airplane is an airplane!

I sweat in the icy air. Can I make it? Would I succeed?

Meet the challenge! Ride the river, the voice in my head pleads. *Decide now. Use your potential. Use your desire. Succeed!*

"OK, OK, I'll do it," I shout to the wind and snow and noise. "I'll do it!"

I turn toward the mountain once more. Catching the river, we climb—an airplane in an elevator of air. I move closer to the frozen skin of my challenge, searching for the lift generated by the rushing currents flowing along the rugged contours of the mountain's face. Up, up, up we rise, higher than birds care to fly, higher than most men dream, higher than fear can reach.

The wings strain to capture every gust, every lifting breath that nature offers.

The air in the cockpit is cold, but I don't notice. I must concentrate on the mountain, the wind, the airplane. The summit looms above me. I hug the mountain as close as I dare. I know that my river will follow the curve of snow and ice at the top and immediately begin a rushing, falling, crashing descent on the other side. I must fly out of the river at just the right moment or be carried down with it.

Now! The summit drifts past my wing. I slam the control stick hard right and tramp down on the rudder pedal. My little airplane labors to move away from the mountain as the river that brought us to the top tumbles down the eastern slope. We're thrown into the still, thin air surrounding the crest.

I level my wings and run, allowing my craft to descend naturally as it seeks the denser air below us. After a minute or two, I slowly turn to face my victory. Shasta stares at me, eye to eye, beautiful, majestic, conquered.

I want to stay, but I must seek the thicker, oxygen-rich atmosphere of lower altitudes. We continue our glide toward the valley far, far below.

For the first time in what seems like an eternity, I breathe a long, relaxed breath. My body is weak and spent but happy. Using unseen forces beyond our control, my little airplane and I have climbed the mountain and crossed the summit. We've claimed the victory, leaving fear to flounder in the foothills.